TO:
FROM:
DATE:

Wild Hope

ONE STEP CLOSER

Wild Hope

CANDACE CAMERON BURE

ZONDERVAN

ZONDERVAN

Wild Hope

Published by Zondervan, 3950 Sparks Drive SE, Suite 101, Grand Rapids, Michigan 49546, USA. Zondervan is a registered trademark of The Zondervan Corporation, L.L.C., a wholly owned subsidiary of HarperCollins Christian Publishing, Inc. Requests for information should be addressed to customercare@harpercollins.com.

ISBN 978-0-310-46637-6 (HC)

Art direction: Tiffany Forrester
Interior design: Lori Lynch

Printed in India

26 27 28 29 30 REP 10 9 8 7 6 5 4 3 2 1

Contents

A NOTE FROM *Candace*

INTRODUCTION

How would you live if you had hope that never failed—even on your hardest day? How would your life be different if you *knew*, down in the deepest part of you, that God loves you? And that His love will never fail?

Please hear this, friend: God is *with* you. He is *for* you. And because of this, no matter what, you can rely on Him.

In fact, nothing in all creation can separate you from God's love for you (Romans 8:38–39). Nothing can snatch you out of His hand (John 10:28). He will always cherish you, care for you, strengthen you, and keep you close to His heart. He has so many good things—and *great* things—in store for you!

From my own life and the stories of others, I've learned that—although we have our shining moments—many of us wrestle with our brokenness daily. We battle feelings of guilt, failure, and frustration, of unworthiness, hopelessness, and despair.

Sometimes the challenges we face are extraordinarily difficult, even excruciating. We may find ourselves dealing with overwhelming trauma, grief, loss, and pain. But more often, our challenges are the ordinary kind—the little letdowns, irritations, and frustrations found in each day—that wear us down over time, gradually eroding or weakening our faith.

Whatever season you find yourself in, I think you'll agree with me about this: We need all the hope and encouragement we can get! And we can find hope when we look for it.

Wild hope can be found in all kinds of places:

In God's promises.
In the dreams hidden in our hearts.
In the love of our family and friends.
In the joy of laughter.
In the beauty of nature.
In the midst of storms as well as in sunshine.
In the grace of forgiveness.
In the kindness of strangers.
In the dawn of a new day.
In the courage to try again.

We can experience this hope, grab ahold of this hope, and live in the power of this wild hope every single day.

You may be saying, "Candace, that sounds like more than hope; it sounds like an impossible dream!"

Friend, it's not always easy to believe, but I've learned that we can become courageous when we have this kind of wild hope—the hope that comes from knowing that with God, all things are possible (Matthew 19:26), that God always keeps His promises, and that He fulfills every one of His good plans and purposes for us.

How about if we discover what it means to live with wild hope for thirty days—together?

To move us one step closer to becoming the spiritually whole and healthy women we've been created to be, I've packed thirty days' worth of inspiration inside these pages. That means you can begin today! You don't need a seminary degree or a church background to join me. You don't even have to own a Bible. Just bring along something to write with and a willing spirit, and you're covered. This devotional guide will equip you with the encouragement you need to succeed: the power of Scripture, devotional readings from my heart to yours, guided questions where we'll explore the challenges we each face, and lots of creative exercises for taking action to overcome them! Together we'll discover many ways God calls us to cultivate a wild hope. The more we focus our hearts and minds on His truths, the more inspired and empowered we'll be to answer His call.

The Bible tells us that our God is the ultimate source of everlasting, eternal hope—and that He will fill us to overflowing with joy and peace as we trust in Him (Romans 15:13). Because He lives in us and works through us, we can have courage and confidence that can't be shaken. We can take on anything that comes our way.

Let's start *today*!

In this together,

Candace

A QUICK Q&A FROM CANDACE

Wherever you are on your spiritual journey, I want you to know you're not alone. We all have questions about God and faith, so I've answered some questions people typically ask me about my Christian faith. I hope these answers will be helpful to you too.

WHY SHOULD I READ AND STUDY THE BIBLE?

The Bible is full of history, wisdom, guidelines, and poetry, but as a whole, it's actually the epic story of all creation since the beginning of time. In the Bible, God is the ultimate Storyteller, sharing His plan and His design for the world and for humanity. No other book is so transformational because no other book shows us how much we are loved by our Creator.

WHAT DOES IT MEAN TO BE "SAVED"?

When followers of Jesus talk about being saved, we mean that Jesus rescued us from the ultimate consequence of sin: eternal separation from God. When we continually choose our way rather than God's way, we become filled with darkness, hopelessness, shame, guilt, and fear. Being saved means acknowledging that we are sinful and need God's forgiveness and that Jesus died on the cross as payment for our sins. We acknowledge that Jesus is the way, and He shines His light, freedom, joy, peace, and hope into our lives.

WHAT IF I DON'T THINK I NEED TO BE SAVED?

I understand this one. You're trying to be a good person. Why do you need to be "saved," right? But we have to realize that God's standards are different from human standards. If we just compare ourselves to other people, it's easy to think we're good enough. But when we compare ourselves to God's standards, we fall miserably short. Every. Single. Time. But because God loves us, He sent His Son, Jesus, to die so that every person—no matter what they've done or where they come from—could be fully forgiven and have a loving relationship with Him.

IS THERE REALLY ONLY ONE WAY TO GOD?

This is a tough one for a lot of people, but the short answer is yes. There is only one way to God, and it's through Jesus Christ. Jesus didn't say, "I am one of the ways to God." Jesus said, "I am the way, the truth, and the life. No one can come to the Father except through me" (John 14:6). He's it. He's the only way.

Though this idea may seem very narrow, it's actually quite comforting. Many religions teach people to work to earn good standing with God. With Jesus, being right with God doesn't depend on what we do or don't do. It depends on what Jesus has already done: He died on the cross to take the punishment for our sins, and then He rose again to give us life with Him. All we must do is acknowledge our sinfulness, ask God for His forgiveness, and then accept His gift of salvation. Then we get to spend our lives loving Him.

HOW CAN I HAVE A RELATIONSHIP WITH GOD?

If you ask God how to find Him, He will make it very clear to you. One way to strengthen your bond with your heavenly Father is simply to talk to Him. Tell Him your worries, fears, concerns, doubts, hopes, and dreams. Tell Him all of it! A prayer doesn't need to be long or eloquent. Your physical posture or volume don't make prayer more or less effective. God says that when you pray, "be sure that your faith is in God alone" (James 1:6).

As you pray, listen for God's voice. How do you know when God is speaking to you? God speaks to us in different ways, and He'll never say something that contradicts what the Bible teaches. When I'm reading certain verses and my heart flip-flops, I know God is showing me something important and I should pay attention.

God will also speak to us through friends, pastors, and teachers. He may even reveal Himself to us through nature or certain circumstances. Just be open to however He wants to speak to you.

HOW DO I USE THIS DEVOTIONAL GUIDE?

I love this devotional guide because it encourages you to experience the life-changing message of God's Word for yourself. Each of the thirty entries includes the following:

- **Scripture**

  Each entry starts with Scripture passages that address what it means to live with wild, unshakable hope. God's Word tells us how to find that hope in Him. Be sure to read each verse, say the words out loud, and maybe even memorize the verses so you can repeat them back to yourself when you need an extra shot of hope, courage, and faith.

- **A Note from Candace**

  I love telling people about the many ways God has filled my life with hope. In these entries, I share some real-life moments when I've leaned on my Savior for help and hope to remind you that God wants to help you too—with anything, at any time, in any place. Nothing is impossible for Him! It's taken me a long time to understand this (and let's face it, I still forget a lot), but it's true! He's got this!

- **Think on It**

  Your turn! It's time to answer a few questions about how you're feeling and who you are becoming. Sometimes answers will come quickly, and sometimes you may have to do some soul-searching; either way, the exercise of writing it down will help you acknowledge and focus on where you are in your spiritual journey. Be honest! This is your safe place.

- **Act on It**

  I want you to think outside the box, so every entry includes a different interactive activity such as filling in a list, shading in boxes, adding to a chart—various ways to help you find a fresh perspective on the topic at hand.

I hope that during this thirty-day journey—through the Scripture passages, testimonies, questions, and activities—you'll find yourself letting go of discouragement, doubt, and fear. As you nurture the wild hope that comes from knowing God is with you, you'll rise up with new courage, believing you have everything you need. Because *He* is all you need.

ONLINE COMPANION COURSE

Want more? I created an online companion course for you! Scan the QR code with a mobile device to see how you can join me for exclusive Scripture readings, stories, and a community where you can connect with other readers.

LET'S DO THIS!

I'm thrilled that we are embarking on this journey together. We are about to learn what wild hope is—what it looks like and where it can be found. We will also find out what this kind of hope can do for us, in us, and through us. Remember, God plants this hope in our hearts. It comes from Him. And with His help, we can grow and nurture this hope until it becomes unshakable and unstoppable. Do you know what's amazing about having this hope? We don't have to just survive; we can also thrive—even through adversity—as we embrace the great adventure of God's calling on our lives. No matter what comes our way, we can be confident that God is with us and is for us.

Before we get started, let's say this little prayer and ask God to be with us in the process.

Dear God, be with me during this thirty-day journey. I want to be closer to You. You know, Lord, that sometimes I get disappointed and discouraged. I feel weary and worn out, frustrated and hopeless. Help me to believe that You are with me and that You will redeem and restore every part of me. Show me what I need to learn to grow closer to You. Shine Your light on the topics in this book that I need to understand more deeply, and help me to live with a wild, fierce hope in You. In Jesus's name, amen.

Day
1

Hope Is Wild *and* Unexpected

God can do anything, you know—far more than you could ever imagine or guess or request in your wildest dreams!

EPHESIANS 3:20 THE MESSAGE

We also celebrate in seasons of suffering because we know that when we suffer we develop endurance, which shapes our characters. When our characters are refined, we learn what it means to hope and anticipate God's goodness. *And hope will never fail to satisfy our deepest need because the Holy Spirit that was given to us has flooded our hearts with God's love.*

ROMANS 5:3–5 THE VOICE

Ephesians 1:11–12
THE MESSAGE

It's in Christ that we find out who we are and what we are living for. Long before we first heard of Christ and got our hopes up, he had his eye on us, had designs on us for glorious living, part of the overall purpose he is working out in everything and everyone.

2 Corinthians 3:12
THE MESSAGE

With that kind of hope to excite us, nothing holds us back.

Romans 12:10–12
AMP

Be devoted to one another . . . aglow in the Spirit, enthusiastically serving the Lord; constantly rejoicing in hope [because of our confidence in Christ], steadfast and patient in distress, devoted to prayer [continually seeking wisdom, guidance, and strength].

1 Corinthians 13:7
AMP

Love bears all things [regardless of what comes], believes all things [looking for the best in each one], hopes all things [remaining steadfast during difficult times], endures all things [without weakening].

Hebrews 6:11–12
THE MESSAGE

I want each of you to extend that same intensity toward a full-bodied hope, and keep at it till the finish. Don't drag your feet. Be like those who stay the course with committed faith and then get everything promised to them.

A NOTE FROM *Candace*

Hope Is Wild and Unexpected

Merriam-Webster's Dictionary defines *hope* as "to expect with confidence" or "to want something to happen or be true."

The phrase *wild hope* takes this definition to another level.

Wild hope is being confident in the God of hope—the God who can do so much more than we expect, so much more than we can ask for, so much more than we can dream or imagine (Ephesians 3:20).

Wild hope is expecting the God of miracles to act—the God who moves mightily and miraculously in our hearts and lives as well as in the lives of our loved ones and others in the world.

Wild hope doesn't have safety rails. It doesn't need a backup plan. It firmly believes in divine intervention—that God can and will step in to do what only He can do.

When the Bible tells us to hope in God, it's not suggesting the spiritual equivalent of wishing on a star. It's telling us to trust in God—in who God is and what He has promised us. We can trust in the great love He has for us, no matter what.

The truth is, life doesn't always work out the way we plan. It can be tough. We may face some hardship and heartache and pain.

But with wild hope, we know that even when bad things happen, God is still with us. He still loves us and cares for us. And we know He has a plan for our lives.

Wild hope says He will use even *this*—whatever *this* is—for His glory and our good.

And our hearts will be glad.

We will rejoice again and again! We will celebrate the goodness of God in the land of the living (Psalm 27:13).

And if you can't see it yet, if you're not quite feeling it, hang in there and hope in the Lord.

"Wait for and confidently expect the LORD; be strong and let your heart take courage; yes, wait for and confidently expect the LORD" (Psalm 27:14 AMP).

Let's do it together!

think on it

What does "wild hope" mean to you? How would you define it or describe it?

What do you think wild hope looks like in real life? What images or examples come to mind?

What would you like to learn about this kind of hope? What questions do you have about it?

think on it

Have you ever had a season in life when you had a wild hope in God? If so, how did having that kind of hope make you feel? What did it inspire you to do?

Think of someone in your life who embodies the kind of wild hope you want to have. Why do you think you've noticed their wild hope? How do you think their wild hope has helped them?

What do you hope will happen in your heart and life over the next thirty days? How do you want wild hope to change you?

Act on It

The psalmist prayed, "Lead me by your truth and teach me, for you are the God who saves me. All day long I put my hope in you" (Psalm 25:5). Write your own prayer, expressing what's in your heart as we begin this adventure together.

I KNOW WHAT I'M DOING. I HAVE IT ALL PLANNED OUT—PLANS TO TAKE CARE OF YOU, NOT ABANDON YOU, PLANS TO GIVE YOU THE FUTURE YOU HOPE FOR.

JEREMIAH 29:11 THE MESSAGE

Day
2

Hope Is Fresh *and* New

Anyone who belongs to Christ has become a new person. The old life is gone; a new life has begun!

2 CORINTHIANS 5:17

May you have the power to understand, as all God's people should, how wide, how long, how high, and how deep his love is.

EPHESIANS 3:18

Ephesians 3:19
AMP

[That you may come] to know [practically, through personal experience] the love of Christ which far surpasses [mere] knowledge [without experience], that you may be filled up [throughout your being] to all the fullness of God [so that you may have the richest experience of God's presence in your lives, completely filled and flooded with God Himself].

Ephesians 4:23–24
THE MESSAGE

Then take on an entirely new way of life—a God-fashioned life, a life renewed from the inside and working itself into your conduct as God accurately reproduces his character in you.

Colossians 3:10–11

Put on your new nature, and be renewed as you learn to know your Creator and become like him. In this new life . . . Christ is all that matters, and he lives in all of us.

1 Peter 4:19

Keep on doing what is right, and trust your lives to the God who created you, for he will never fail you.

Lamentations 3:22–23

The faithful love of the LORD never ends! His mercies never cease. Great is his faithfulness; his mercies begin afresh each morning.

A NOTE FROM *Candace*

Hope Is Fresh and New

Many people think I grew up in a Christian home, but I didn't. I grew up in a moral home, a home that stressed the importance of living by the Golden Rule. But it wasn't until my parents hit a hard place in their marriage that the four of us kids found ourselves in church. It was the beginning of a new life for our whole family. That's where I first met Jesus and was baptized when I was twelve.

But my teenage years were busy, and going to church became less of a priority for me. I remember thinking that since God lived inside my heart, I could talk to Him anytime (which is true), so I didn't really need to go to church to help me grow in my faith (which is *not* true!). Instead of having a relationship with Jesus, I considered Him more of a helpline I'd call in case of an emergency.

Whenever I felt a twinge of guilt or a conviction about something I was doing, I would compare myself to others my age. I was still a good kid, I was fairly responsible, and I liked pleasing my parents. Unlike other child stars, I didn't get into drugs or alcohol or trouble with the law. My life seemed pretty tame. I tried to focus on times I was kind or generous, and on other good deeds I thought would tip the "good versus evil" scale in my favor. I remember thinking, *Is this really how God works? Can I just do whatever I want and then ask for forgiveness later? How good do I* really *have to be?*

Then I learned that God's standard of goodness is different from the world's standard, and for the first time I saw myself as a sinner. For the first time I really understood that despite all the good I did, whenever I did something that was wrong or hurt someone else, I had broken God's law. I also recognized that Jesus paid the penalty for my sin with His own life, and there is no love greater than that in the whole universe. He rescued me, He saved me, He delivered me—and knowing this led me to real repentance and a heart change. Out of gratitude for what Jesus did for me, I now genuinely want to live a life that honors His sacrifice. A life that pleases Him. A life that points others to Him.

It's been many years since I began this new adventure, this new life in Christ. I'm still learning what it means to live my life for Him. I'm still learning and growing in my relationship with Him.

Sometimes I make mistakes or lose my way. But my hope is not to get to a place where I do it all perfectly on my own, or to do enough good to outweigh the bad. My hope is in Jesus and what He's already done for me. My hope is in His unconditional love for me. My hope is in His forgiveness, His amazing mercy and grace—which are fresh and new each and every day.

think on it

In John 10:10, Jesus says He came so that we could have "real and eternal life" (THE MESSAGE). What do you think that kind of life looks like?

Think about who you were before you knew Jesus. How has knowing Jesus changed the way you live?

How has the trap of comparison kept you from seeing God's standard over the world's standard?

think on it

In what ways do you think your life points others to God?

First John 1:8–10 reminds us: "If we claim that we're free of sin, we're only fooling ourselves. A claim like that is errant nonsense. On the other hand, if we admit our sins—simply come clean about them—he won't let us down; he'll be true to himself. He'll forgive our sins and purge us of all wrongdoing" (THE MESSAGE). Is there anything in your heart that you need to confess today? Where in your life do you need God's forgiveness, mercy, and grace?

In Psalm 51, David confessed his sins before God and prayed, "Create in me a new, clean heart, O God, filled with clean thoughts and right desires" (v. 10 TLB). Write a prayer in your own words, asking God to help you cultivate a new, clean heart.

Act on It

Philippians 1:6 says, "I am sure that God who began the good work within you will keep right on helping you grow in his grace until his task within you is finally finished on that day when Jesus Christ returns" (TLB).

In the space below, write the timeline of your journey of faith so far. Highlight the happy moments of your journey, and don't be shy about including moments when you messed up or endured something hard. As you revisit these darker moments, see if you can find where God gave you fresh, new hope.

GOD, WHO GOT YOU STARTED IN THIS SPIRITUAL ADVENTURE . . . WILL NEVER GIVE UP ON YOU. NEVER FORGET THAT.

1 CORINTHIANS 1:8–9 THE MESSAGE

Day
3

Hope Is Alive *and* Eternal

That faith and that knowledge come from our hope for life forever. God promised that life to us before time began.

TITUS 1:2 ICB

Blessed [gratefully praised and adored] be the God and Father of our Lord Jesus Christ, who according to His abundant and boundless mercy has caused us to be born again [that is, to be reborn from above—spiritually transformed, renewed, and set apart for His purpose] to an ever-living hope and confident assurance through the resurrection of Jesus Christ from the dead.

1 PETER 1:3 AMP

1 Peter 1:4–5
THE MESSAGE

Because Jesus was raised from the dead, we've been given a brand-new life and have everything to live for, including a future in heaven—and the future starts now! God is keeping careful watch over us and the future. The Day is coming when you'll have it all—life healed and whole.

Titus 3:7
ICB

We were made right with God by His grace. And God gave us the Spirit so that we could receive the life that never ends. That is what we hope for.

Titus 2:12
THE VOICE

Grace arrives with its own instruction: run away from anything that leads us away from God . . . live life now in this age *with awareness* and self-control, doing the right thing and keeping yourselves holy.

Titus 2:13
AMP

Awaiting and confidently expecting the [fulfillment of our] blessed hope and the glorious appearing of our great God and Savior, Christ Jesus.

2 Thessalonians 2:15–17
THE MESSAGE

Friends, take a firm stand, feet on the ground and head high. Keep a tight grip on what you were taught, whether in personal conversation or by our letter. May Jesus himself and God our Father, who reached out in love and surprised you with gifts of unending help and confidence, put a fresh heart in you, invigorate your work, enliven your speech.

Hebrews 10:23
THE MESSAGE

Let's keep a firm grip on the promises that keep us going. He always keeps his word.

Hope Is Alive and Eternal

Maybe you've heard this expression: "Hope springs eternal!" It's true. Wild hope is a living, eternal hope that never gives in, never gives up, and never dies.

Sometimes this hope may seem to fade, falter, or go quiet for a while. Sometimes it may seem like it's gone underground—like a seed or a spring of water. But then, all of a sudden, it's bubbling up again! Sometimes when we least expect it, wild hope bursts forth with new life and new growth, just in time for a brand-new season.

Why does hope act this way? Because the ultimate Source of hope is always alive and well. The Bible describes this source as "Christ in you, the hope of glory" (Colossians 1:27 KJV). Jesus is always loving us, living in us, and working through us and for us—which gives us hope. Different translations of 1 Timothy 1:1 describe Him as "our living hope" (THE MESSAGE), "our *living and certain* hope" (THE VOICE), and "our only hope" (TLB).

This hope can't be killed by criticism or ridicule. It can't be killed by negativity, by fear or doubt, by discouragement or even despair. It can't be killed by suffering or pain. It can't even be killed by evil.

I mean, evil tried, but it didn't triumph.

Jesus died, but He rose from the grave.

And because He did, we have this powerful hope that lives forever and ever, living inside us today.

All we have to do is receive it. Embrace it.

Nurture it, nourish it, cultivate it. Protect it.

Hold on to the hope He's given us, and hang on for dear life! And as you do, remember that this living and eternal hope is holding on to us lovingly, faithfully, and tightly.

think on it

Think about a moment or season when you felt your hope had disappeared. Why did you feel that way?

Where did you find hope again? When or how did it come back?

Have you ever tried to find hope in a source that wasn't Jesus? What happened?

think on it

How would you describe your hope today?

The Bible warns us that evil is real and that we have an enemy—a "thief"—whose purpose is "to steal and kill and destroy" (John 10:10). He certainly tries to steal our joy, kill our peace, and destroy our hope. How does the enemy try to rob you of your hope? What lies does he whisper in your ear?

The good news is that we aren't powerless against this enemy. James 4:7 says that if we resist him, he will flee from us. First John 4:4 explains that "you have already won a victory . . . because the Spirit who lives in you is greater than the spirit who lives in the world." The next time you feel defeated, what will you do to remind yourself that you're already victorious?

Act on It

Philippians 4:8–9 says, "Fix your thoughts on what is true, and honorable, and right, and pure, and lovely, and admirable. Think about things that are excellent and worthy of praise. Keep putting into practice all you learned and received. . . . Then the God of peace will be with you."

What can you do to "fix your thoughts on what is true"—to remind yourself that our hope in God is alive and eternal? What new habits do you need to form? What Bible verses do you want to memorize? What changes do you need to make to the music or shows you're streaming? Write your plan down below.

MY HEALTH MAY FAIL, AND MY SPIRIT MAY GROW WEAK, BUT GOD REMAINS THE STRENGTH OF MY HEART; HE IS MINE FOREVER.

PSALM 73:26

Day 4

Hope Is *a* Gift

I do everything to spread the Good News and share in its blessings.

1 CORINTHIANS 9:23

God, who encourages those who are discouraged, encouraged us.

2 CORINTHIANS 7:6

2 Thessalonians 2:16 ICB	Through his grace he gave us a good hope and comfort that continues forever.
Romans 8:24	We were given this hope when we were saved.
2 Timothy 1:7 AMP	God did not give us a spirit of timidity or cowardice or fear, but [He has given us a spirit] of power and of love and of sound judgment and personal discipline [abilities that result in a calm, well-balanced mind and self-control].
Romans 1:12 THE VOICE	I know that when we come together *something beautiful will happen as* we are encouraged by each other's faith.
Romans 1:12 TLB	I want not only to share my faith with you but to be encouraged by yours: Each of us will be a blessing to the other.
1 Corinthians 12:7	A spiritual gift is given to each of us so we can help each other.
Romans 12:6, 8	In his grace, God has given us different gifts for doing certain things well. . . . If your gift is to encourage others, be encouraging.
1 Thessalonians 5:11 THE MESSAGE	So speak encouraging words to one another. Build up hope so you'll all be together in this, no one left out, no one left behind.

A NOTE FROM
Candace

Hope Is a Gift

There's only one reason I can get up in the morning and breathe. Only one reason I can keep going, day after day. Only one reason I can accomplish anything.

The gift of hope I have in Jesus.

Come to think of it, everything in my life is a gift from God. This life is a gift. The air we breathe is a gift. Our talents and abilities are gifts. Our relationships are gifts. Our resources are gifts.

Our hope is one of God's greatest gifts to us. He gave us this hope when He gave us salvation—because when we were lost in our sin and separated from Him, He loved us and sent His Son to be our Savior.

Not only does God give us the hope of heaven, our true home, and the perfect life there that never ends, but He also gives us hope for *this* life, right here and now, in all its brokenness. He helps us find healing. He helps us find meaning and purpose, grace and strength, love and joy and peace.

It's all a gift from God.

That's why I can't stop talking about Him! It's why I share Him with as many people in as many ways as I can. Sometimes people compliment me on my boldness or courage on social media—how publicly I live out my faith—and their kind words bless me.

But honestly, I don't see how I could live any other way! I've been given a platform, a position of influence, and I want to use it to share what's most important to me.

First Peter 3:15–16 says, "Worship Christ as Lord of your life. And if someone asks about your hope as a believer, always be ready to explain it. But do this in a gentle and respectful way."

That's what I try to do. Gently, yes. Lovingly, yes. But also faithfully and honestly and unashamedly. Because I want to give others the hope that has been given to me—the hope of the gospel, the good news of Jesus. This hope is so real, so true, so powerful, so life-changing for me. I know it will be for them too.

think on it

When life is hard, how does your hope in Jesus help you get up in the morning and face the day?

What have you seen God do in your life that has affirmed the wild hope you have in Him?

How has God's wild hope been a life-changing gift for you?

think on it

Who first shared the good news with you? Who gives you hope or encourages you in your life today?

Each of us has some kind of platform or position of influence, some specific roles or relationships that give us opportunities—big or small—to share hope with those around us. What opportunities has God given you? How can you pass along the gift you have received?

In 2 Corinthians 4:5–7, the apostle Paul wrote, "Remember, our Message is not about ourselves; we're proclaiming Jesus Christ, the Master. All we are is messengers, errand runners from Jesus for you. . . . We carry this precious Message around in the unadorned clay pots of our ordinary lives. That's to prevent anyone from confusing God's incomparable power with us" (THE MESSAGE). Think about the phrase "unadorned clay pots" and how this scripture directs us to share the good news of Jesus with others. How does it feel knowing that God doesn't expect us to share His gift of hope perfectly?

Act on It

In the Bible, Paul described himself—and us—as being messengers "on special assignment" to share the good news with others, "holding out and offering to everyone the word of life" (2 Timothy 1:1 THE MESSAGE; Philippians 2:16 AMP).

First, pray and ask God to give you a "special assignment" this week. Ask Him to bring to mind a person to whom you can give the gift of hope and encouragement, or a situation where you can shine His light and share His love.

Next, take a little time to brainstorm some of the ways you might do this. Come up with a plan you can put into action and write it down below. (Remember: Be open to additional assignments or spur-of-the-moment inspiration!)

HOW BEAUTIFUL ON THE MOUNTAINS ARE THE FEET OF THE MESSENGER BRINGING GOOD NEWS.

ISAIAH 52:7 THE MESSAGE

Day 5

Hope Is Fierce

God, a most fierce warrior, is at my side.

JEREMIAH 20:11 THE MESSAGE

I pray that from his glorious, unlimited resources he will empower you with inner strength through his Spirit.

EPHESIANS 3:16

Psalm 31:24 THE MESSAGE	Be brave. Be strong. Don't give up. Expect GOD to get here soon.
Job 11:18	Having hope will give you courage. You will be protected.
Psalm 46:1–3 THE MESSAGE	God is a safe place to hide, ready to help when we need him. We stand fearless at the cliff-edge of doom, courageous in seastorm and earthquake, before the rush and roar of oceans, the tremors that shift mountains. . . . God fights for us, GOD-of-Angel-Armies protects us.
Deuteronomy 31:6	Be strong and courageous! Do not be afraid and do not panic before them. For the LORD your God will personally go ahead of you. He will neither fail you nor abandon you.
Psalm 16:1	Keep me safe, O God, for I have come to you for refuge.
Psalm 18:39	You have armed me with strength for the battle.
Isaiah 8:17 THE MESSAGE	I stand my ground and hope.
Psalm 145:4 THE MESSAGE	Generation after generation stands in awe of your work; each one tells stories of your mighty acts.

A NOTE FROM *Candace*

Hope Is Fierce

As a public figure, I've been blessed with a platform that has given me many opportunities to share my faith with others—to point them to the Savior, who means everything to me. I'm grateful that in interviews and on social media, I get a chance to offer a Christian perspective or take a stand on important issues.

Speaking these truths in public isn't always easy. I don't always do it perfectly. But I try my best to honor God in every situation. Sometimes the response is really positive! Sometimes it's not. Over the years I've received plenty of negative feedback, criticism, and ridicule. Taking a stand for God has cost me some friendships. It's cost me in my career. Yet I know these sacrifices have been so small compared to the sacrifices others have been called to make.

I guess that's why one of my favorite stories in all of Scripture is the story of Esther. Esther was an orphaned Jewish girl miraculously chosen to be queen of Persia. When she learned of a plot to annihilate the Jewish people living in the empire, she was challenged to stand up and speak out—to approach her notoriously temperamental husband, King Xerxes, and ask for his help. But appearing before Xerxes without an invitation literally could have cost Esther her life.

Esther's story gives me hope because *she* had hope in God—even in the most overwhelming circumstance. She had faith that God could—and would—come to her rescue, that He would deliver her and her people.

That hope made her fierce. It made her bold and courageous, willing to put her own life on the line for others. Willing to sacrifice herself, if necessary. Hope led her to pray—fervently, passionately, persistently. And God answered her prayers.

He gave Esther the wisdom and discernment to navigate an incredibly difficult situation. He showed her how and when to stand up and speak out. He gave her favor with the king. He saved her and all her people with her.

And the most amazing thing? The same God who filled Esther with fierce hope and courageous faith is with you and me today. Whenever He calls us to take a stand, He stands with us. He gives us the words to speak. He leads us and guides us, protects us and defends us. He answers our prayers.

We live in hope because we know our lives are safe in His hands.

think on it

In 1 Peter 2:9 we read, "You are a chosen people. You are royal priests, a holy nation, God's very own possession. As a result, you can show others the goodness of God, for he called you out of the darkness into his wonderful light." And in 1 Thessalonians 1:4, Paul said to those who follow Jesus, "It is clear to us, friends, that God not only loves you very much but also has put his hand on you for something special" (THE MESSAGE). Do you have a sense of God's calling in your life? He may call you to a specific career or location, but He calls everyone to show others His goodness. How can you share that goodness today?

Esther was challenged and inspired by the words of her cousin Mordecai, who asked this question: "Who knows but that you have come to your royal position for such a time as this?" (Esther 4:14 NIV). Have you ever felt that God brought you to a certain moment so He could use you? If not, think about the gifts God has given to you. How might God use your gifts to do good in the world?

Think about your position of influence—the roles or responsibilities you have in your family, your school or workplace, your church or community. How are you impacting the people around you with your words and actions?

think on it

How might God be asking you to take a stand, to show up, or to speak out? When and where might you need to do that?

Was there a time you thought about speaking out but didn't? How did you feel afterward? What do you wish you would've done differently?

Ephesians 4:1 urges us to "live a life worthy of the calling to which you have been called [that is, to live a life that exhibits godly character, moral courage, personal integrity, and mature behavior—a life that expresses gratitude to God for your salvation]" (AMP). How does this verse inspire you to fiercely live a life of godly hope?

Act on It

The Bible tells us that God has special "armor" for us to wear—spiritual gear that protects us and equips us for battle:

> Be strong in the Lord and in his mighty power. . . . Put on every piece of God's armor so you will be able to resist the enemy in the time of evil. Then after the battle you will still be standing firm. Stand your ground, putting on the belt of truth and the body armor of God's righteousness. For shoes, put on the peace that comes from the Good News so that you will be fully prepared. In addition to all of these, hold up the shield of faith to stop the fiery arrows of the devil. Put on salvation as your helmet, and take the sword of the Spirit, which is the word of God. Pray in the Spirit at all times and on every occasion. Stay alert and be persistent in your prayers. (Ephesians 6:10, 13–18)

Which piece of God's armor do you need the most today? Write a prayer asking God to help you put on this piece of armor and live fiercely devoted to Him.

BE ON GUARD. STAND FIRM IN THE FAITH.

BE COURAGEOUS. BE STRONG.

1 CORINTHIANS 16:13

Day

6

Hope Is True

When doubts fill my mind, when my heart is in turmoil, quiet me and give me renewed hope and cheer.

PSALM 94:19 TLB

Why am I so overwrought? Why am I so disturbed? Why can't I just hope in God? Despite all my emotions, *I will* believe and *praise the One who saves me* and is my life.

PSALM 42:5 THE VOICE

I still dare to hope when I remember this: The faithful love of the LORD never ends! His mercies never cease.

LAMENTATIONS 3:21–22

Micah 7:7
THE VOICE

I will look to the Eternal One, and my hope is in the True God who will save me. My God will hear me.

Psalm 26:12

Now I stand on solid ground, and I will publicly praise the LORD.

Hebrews 6:17–19
THE MESSAGE

When God wanted to guarantee his promises, he gave his word, a rock-solid guarantee—God *can't* break his word. And because his word cannot change, the promise is likewise unchangeable. We who have run for our very lives to God have every reason to grab the promised hope with both hands and never let go. It's an unbreakable spiritual lifeline, reaching past all appearances right to the very presence of God.

1 Corinthians 13:13
THE MESSAGE

Trust steadily in God, hope unswervingly, love extravagantly.

Psalm 130:7
THE VOICE

Ground your hope in the Eternal. For in the Eternal lives *the most* loyal love, and with Him comes *the most* abundant redemption.

A NOTE FROM
Candace

Hope Is True

We all wrestle with worry and fear. We all have moments when doubt and discouragement creep in—when we look around and can't see the positive, can't find the good, can't feel the love.

We want to live a life of adventure, a life of faith, a life full of wild hope—but suddenly the idea seems like a fairy tale. All of it.

That's when we have to remember that our hope isn't just a feeling. (You'll learn more about this on day 7.) And that's a good thing, because you know how often feelings change! It doesn't come from ourselves, our thoughts or imaginations, our strengths or skills, our abilities or resources. And hope doesn't come from our best friend or our significant other either.

Our hope isn't make-believe.

It's real.

It's true.

It has been from the very beginning.

Because our hope is in Jesus.

We learn about Him from the stories in the Bible, from people who actually met Him in the flesh. Here's what they said when they were talking about Jesus's promise to be with us always and to come back to earth again after He left:

> We weren't, you know, just wishing on a star when we laid the facts out before you regarding the powerful return of our Master, Jesus Christ. We were there for the preview! We saw it with our own eyes: Jesus resplendent with light from God the Father as the voice of Majestic Glory spoke: "This is my Son, marked by my love, focus of all my delight." We were there on the holy mountain with him. We heard the voice out of heaven with our very own ears. (2 Peter 1:16–18 THE MESSAGE)

Those first disciples of Jesus—and all the disciples who have lived in the two thousand years since—testify that He is real. He is true. He is faithful to do what He says He will do.

They staked their lives on it. And we can too.

There's a powerful prayer in 2 Thessalonians 2:16–17: "Now may our Lord Jesus Christ Himself and God our Father, who has loved us and given us everlasting comfort and encouragement and the good [well-founded] hope [of salvation] by His grace, comfort and encourage and strengthen your hearts [keeping them steadfast and on course] in every good work and word" (AMP). How do these verses describe the God we're praying to?

How has God given you comfort, encouragement, and hope recently?

Based off what you've already learned about wild hope, why do you think 2 Thessalonians 2:16 describes our hope as "well-founded"?

think on it

What personal experience has confirmed that your hope in God is true?

Who in your life is always testifying about what God has done for them? How does this person inspire you?

What does wild, well-founded hope in God empower you to do? What new action will you take to share this hope?

Act on It

Write a letter to your younger self at a time when you felt hopeless. Tell yourself about what you've learned about God's faithfulness and how He cared for you during this dark time. Tell your younger self why you now know that your hope in God is true.

WE WHO HAVE FLED TO HIM FOR REFUGE CAN HAVE GREAT CONFIDENCE AS WE HOLD TO THE HOPE THAT LIES BEFORE US. THIS HOPE IS A STRONG AND TRUSTWORTHY ANCHOR FOR OUR SOULS.

HEBREWS 6:18–19

Day

7

Hope Is More Than *a* Feeling

Put your hope in the LORD—now and always.

PSALM 131:3

My sad life's dilapidated, a falling-down barn; build me up again by your Word. Barricade the road that goes Nowhere; grace me with your clear revelation. I choose the true road to Somewhere, I post your road signs at every curve and corner. I grasp and cling to whatever you tell me.

PSALM 119:28–31 THE MESSAGE

Psalm 16:5
THE MESSAGE

My choice is you, GOD, first and only. And now I find I'm *your* choice!

Lamentations 3:19–24
THE MESSAGE

I'll never forget the trouble, the utter lostness, the taste of ashes, the poison I've swallowed. I remember it all—oh, how well I remember—the feeling of hitting the bottom. But there's one other thing I remember, and remembering, I keep a grip on hope: GOD's loyal love couldn't have run out, his merciful love couldn't have dried up. They're created new every morning. How great your faithfulness! I'm sticking with GOD (I say it over and over). He's all I've got left.

Psalm 18:6

In my distress I cried out to the LORD; yes, I prayed to my God for help. He heard me from his sanctuary; my cry to him reached his ears.

Psalm 34:6

In my desperation I prayed, and the LORD listened; he saved me from all my troubles.

2 Corinthians 4:16
THE MESSAGE

We're not giving up. How could we! Even though on the outside it often looks like things are falling apart on us, on the inside, where God is making new life, not a day goes by without his unfolding grace.

A NOTE FROM Candace

Hope Is More Than a Feeling

I'm a pretty positive person by nature. Cheerful, upbeat, optimistic—that's me! Somehow, looking for the bright side of things has always come naturally. It's just the way God made me.

But I've had my moments—times when I've felt truly and utterly hopeless, when I've felt incredibly frustrated or deeply discouraged.

For instance, there were times in my marriage when I didn't think Val and I were going to make it. I didn't want to break the covenant promise I had made before God. But I had done everything I knew to do, and our marriage wasn't working. I shed many tears back then. I felt so helpless, unable to fix it.

I've certainly been frustrated and discouraged as a parent. I've had my share of "mom fails," those moments when I wish I'd made better choices or handled certain situations with my kids differently. I've also been frustrated with some of *their* choices. I've wondered where I went wrong as a parent or what I could do to fix the consequences of their choices—when, of course, that's something only God can do!

And then, as I've said before, being a person of faith in the entertainment industry hasn't always been easy.

In these moments, I remember that hope is more than a feeling; hope is a choice, a decision I can make. I can *choose* to hope, even when I don't *feel* hopeful.

I can choose to trust God, choose to have faith and believe He will keep His promises—that He will bring good out of everything that happens to me, including the hardest things (Romans 8:28)

I can choose to believe He will work not only in my heart and life but also in the hearts and lives of the people I love.

I can choose to trust God with all my plans, all my hopes and dreams, and all my needs.

Remembering what Jesus said in Matthew 19:26—"With God all things are possible" (NIV)—I can choose to trust God with all the things that seem impossible or overwhelming.

I've learned from experience that choosing hope changes everything.

think on it

Are you a more positive, optimistic, hopeful person by nature? Or are you still learning to choose hope?

How do you think your positive or negative outlook was formed? By family and friends? By habit? By a particular event in your life?

What are your biggest struggles right now? Where do you most need hope?

think on it

The Bible tells us to come to God with all these things, "casting all your cares [all your anxieties, all your worries, and all your concerns, once and for all] on Him, for He cares about you [with deepest affection, and watches over you very carefully]" (1 Peter 5:7 AMP). How does this verse give you hope?

Practically speaking, how can you "cast your cares" on Him? What does that look like for you?

How can you choose—and keep on choosing—hope? What hope-*full* attitude or mindset can you adopt? What hope-*full* action can you take? What hope-*full* words can you speak?

Act on It

Practice choosing hope today! In the space provided, make a list of five hope-filled statements and Bible verses. Then, throughout your day, see how many times you can use the word *hope*—meaning to believe or trust, not just wish—in conversation, texts, emails, or social media posts. (And don't just say the word *hope*—speak words of hope that encourage and uplift others.) Keep a tally of how many times you see hope in action today.

SPEAK ENCOURAGING WORDS TO ONE ANOTHER. BUILD UP HOPE.

1 THESSALONIANS 5:11 THE MESSAGE

Hope Is Healing

He heals the brokenhearted and bandages their wounds.

PSALM 147:3

Return to your fortress, you prisoners of hope; even now
I announce that I will restore twice as much to you.

ZECHARIAH 9:12 NIV

Malachi 4:2

For you who fear my name, the Sun of Righteousness will rise with healing in his wings.

Isaiah 58:8
AMP

Then your light will break out like the dawn, and your healing (restoration, new life) will quickly spring forth; your righteousness will go before you [leading you to peace and prosperity], the glory of the LORD will be your rear guard.

Jeremiah 17:14

O LORD, if you heal me, I will be truly healed; if you save me, I will be truly saved.

Jeremiah 17:14
THE MESSAGE

GOD, pick up the pieces. Put me back together again. You are my praise!

Psalm 10:17

LORD, you know the hopes of the helpless. Surely you will hear their cries and comfort them.

Matthew 5:4
NIV

Blessed are those who mourn, for they will be comforted.

Haggai 2:9
THE MESSAGE

This Temple is going to end up far better than it started out, a glorious beginning but an even more glorious finish: a place in which I will hand out wholeness and holiness.

Hope Is Healing

The threat of starvation during a famine had forced Naomi and her family to leave their homeland of Israel and immigrate to the faraway kingdom of Moab. Everything in that place was strange and new and hard to get used to.

Then after a while, Naomi *did* get used to it. The new land was nothing like home, but she made it work—for the sake of her husband and their two sons. In time, the boys grew up and got married, and Naomi started looking forward to becoming a grandmother.

But suddenly, in a series of tragedies, Naomi's husband died, and then both of her sons died too. She was absolutely devastated. It seemed like everything—and everyone—she cared about had been torn from her life.

In her despair, she changed her name from *Naomi*, which means "pleasant," to *Mara*, which means "bitter." She told her daughters-in-law to start over—to find new husbands and new lives—and move on without her. She had nothing to offer the young women but her grief and pain, so she was going back home to Israel.

Naomi couldn't find any hope in her situation. But hope found her.

Hope came in the form of her daughter-in-law Ruth, who refused to abandon her and promised to make Naomi's God her God too (Ruth 1:16). Ruth had her own heartache to bear and her own challenges to face—especially as she became an immigrant, a foreigner, in Naomi's homeland. But Ruth's love and loyalty meant the world to her mother-in-law. It was Ruth, after all, who would become Naomi's closest friend and companion, and the mother of Naomi's future grandchildren.

The day was coming when Naomi would no longer be imprisoned by her grief and pain; she would become instead a "prisoner of hope," someone captured and kept alive by hope, even in the most unimaginable circumstances. As Scripture says, "You're blessed when you feel you've lost what is most dear to you. Only then can you be embraced by the One most dear to you" (Matthew 5:4 THE MESSAGE).

When Naomi opened her heart to Ruth, she opened her heart to hope. When she opened her heart to hope, she opened her heart to God. And when she opened her heart to God, she found the healing that would set her free.

think on it

What has been your experience of loss, grief, or pain? When has suffering touched your life most deeply?

Where have you found hope amid your heartache? What, specifically, has helped you on your journey to healing?

How have you experienced God's comfort and healing? How has He shown His love for you?

think on it

Proverbs 17:17 says, "A friend loves at all times, and a brother is born for a time of adversity" (NIV). In your darkest moments, who did God send to walk alongside you, and how did that person help you cling to hope?

Second Corinthians 1:3–4 says, "God is our merciful Father and the source of all comfort. He comforts us in all our troubles so that we can comfort others." Who might be the people God has called you to comfort?

How can you use your experience with grief or pain to help others?

Act on It

Psalm 56:8 says, "You keep track of all my sorrows. You have collected all my tears in your bottle. You have recorded each one in your book." Not one of our tears goes unnoticed by God. He truly and deeply feels our pain. He really cares, the Bible tells us, and He comforts us with His love.

In the space below, write about one thing that has led you to tears recently.

This week, find a small, decorative bottle—something you already have or something from a craft store or secondhand shop, such as a vintage-looking perfume bottle or a vase of some kind. Fill it with water or clear beads or pearls to represent tears. Then place it where you'll see it when you need to be reminded of God's healing love. You can also make one as a gift for a friend or family member going through a tough time. Add a tag with the words from Psalm 56:8 or the words from Revelation below.

[GOD] WILL WIPE AWAY EVERY TEAR FROM THEIR EYES.

REVELATION 21:4 AMP

Day 9

Hope Is *a* Person

This is My beloved Son. Listen to Him.

MARK 9:7 THE VOICE

For this is how God loved the world: He gave his one and only Son, so that everyone who believes in him will not perish but have eternal life.

JOHN 3:16

John 3:17
THE MESSAGE

God didn't go to all the trouble of sending his Son merely to point an accusing finger, telling the world how bad it was. He came to help, to put the world right again.

1 John 3:8
THE VOICE

That is why the Son of God came into our world: to destroy the plague of destruction inflicted *on the world* by the diabolical one.

Philippians 2:8
THE MESSAGE

He lived a selfless, obedient life and then died a selfless, obedient death—and the worst kind of death at that—a crucifixion.

Romans 5:7–8
NIV

Very rarely will anyone die for a righteous person, though for a good person someone might possibly dare to die. But God demonstrates his own love for us in this: While we were still sinners, Christ died for us.

1 Peter 2:24
AMP

He personally carried our sins in His body on the cross [willingly offering Himself on it, as on an altar of sacrifice], so that we might die to sin [becoming immune from the penalty and power of sin] and live for righteousness.

1 Peter 1:21
TLB

Because of this, your trust can be in God who raised Christ from the dead and gave him great glory. Now your faith and hope can rest in him alone.

A NOTE FROM Candace

Hope Is a Person

Wild hope is many things. But more than anything, it's a person.

And that person is Jesus.

No Jesus, no hope. None at all.

Know Jesus, know hope—all the hope in the world, and so much more!

His story—*our* story—is not a fairy tale, even though it sounds like one. It's true!

The Bible tells us that God has "rescued us from the kingdom of darkness and transferred us into the Kingdom of his dear Son, who purchased our freedom and forgave our sins" (Colossians 1:13–14).

We used to be prisoners. We were held captive by our own sin and selfishness—not only by the Prince of Darkness, the Evil One. Colossians 2:14–15 explains, "When you were stuck in your old sin-dead life, you were incapable of responding to God. God brought you alive—right along with Christ! Think of it! All sins forgiven, the slate wiped clean, that old arrest warrant canceled and nailed to Christ's cross" (THE MESSAGE). Now we've been set free, and "God leads us from place to place in one perpetual victory parade" (2 Corinthians 2:14 THE MESSAGE).

Think about how beautiful this is! Today we get to follow in the footsteps of Jesus. We get to walk with Him, talk with Him, and learn more about Him each and every day.

And we get to learn to love Him more and more.

The more we do, the more He fills us with Himself—with wild hope—until we're overflowing.

think on it

In Matthew 16:24, Jesus says, "If any of you wants to be my follower, you must give up your own way, take up your cross, and follow me." Luke 9:23 puts it another way: "Anyone who intends to come with me has to let me lead. . . . Don't run from suffering; embrace it. Follow me and I'll show you how. Self-help is no help at all. Self-sacrifice is the way, *my* way, to finding yourself, your true self" (THE MESSAGE). That's the challenge of a lifetime. What does "taking up your cross" mean to you in your life today?

What has it cost you to follow Jesus?

Some of Jesus's first followers decided taking up a cross was too hard, and they left Him. Jesus asked His disciples if they were going to leave Him too. Peter answered, "Lord, to whom shall we go? You [alone] have the words of eternal life [you are our only hope]" (John 6:68 AMP). Who or what are you tempted to turn to when following Jesus becomes hard?

think on it

What has Jesus asked you to let go of or give up? What sacrifices has He asked you to make? What suffering has He asked you to embrace?

What have you gained by "taking up" the cross of Jesus?

Hebrews 12:3 tells us to think about all Jesus suffered for us, all He endured for our sakes, so that we will "not grow weary and lose heart" (NIV). How does this verse help us to hold on to our wild hope?

Act on It

Many symbols represent hope, and we can use many images (even icons, GIFs, or emojis) to express hope too. But to me, the greatest symbol of hope is the cross—because of what Jesus did there for you and for me.

You may already have a cross decorating your home—maybe more than one! Or you probably have a cross-themed mug, T-shirt, necklace, or earrings. You might have a cross on your keychain or hanging from your rearview mirror. And if you're like me, you're so used to the symbol, you don't even notice it anymore.

Right now, grab one of these crosses. (Or if you don't have a cross nearby, look at one on your phone.) Then think about what the cross really means. In the space below, explain what the cross means to you as if you were talking to someone who has never heard of Jesus or the cross.

THE TEACHING ABOUT THE CROSS SEEMS FOOLISH TO THOSE WHO ARE LOST. BUT TO US WHO ARE BEING SAVED IT IS THE POWER OF GOD.

1 CORINTHIANS 1:18 ICB

Day
10

Hope Is Here

I'll stay right here, your good name my hope.

PSALM 52:9 THE MESSAGE

God is our shelter and our strength. When troubles seem near, God is nearer, and He's ready to help. So why run and hide?

PSALM 46:1 THE VOICE

Psalm 46:7	The LORD of Heaven's Armies is here among us; the God of Israel is our fortress.
Psalm 116:9	I walk in the LORD's presence as I live here on earth!
2 Samuel 22:20	He led me to a place of safety; he rescued me because he delights in me.
Psalm 91:2 THE VOICE	My shelter, my *mighty* fortress, my God, I place *all* my trust in You.
Isaiah 43:2–4 THE MESSAGE	Don't be afraid, I've redeemed you. I've called your name. You're mine. When you're in over your head, I'll be there with you. When you're in rough waters, you will not go down. When you're between a rock and a hard place, it won't be a dead end—because I am GOD, your personal God, The Holy of Israel, your Savior. I paid a huge price for you. . . . *That's* how much you mean to me! *That's* how much I love you! I'd sell off the whole world to get you back, trade the creation just for you.
Isaiah 41:13 THE MESSAGE	I, your GOD, have a firm grip on you and I'm not letting go. I'm telling you, "Don't panic. I'm right here to help you."
Hebrews 13:5 NIV	Never will I leave you; never will I forsake you.
Matthew 28:20	Be sure of this: I am with you always, even to the end of the age.

A NOTE FROM *Candace*

Hope Is Here

Can I share something with you? I really believe hope isn't a wish, a dream, or a far-off fantasy. Hope is real. Hope is true. And hope is here—right now—with you.

Whatever you're going through.

Whatever you're looking forward to.

Whatever your plans or dreams.

Whatever your worries or fears.

Hope is here—because the God of hope is here. He is always with you. And He is for you (Romans 8:31)! He is on your side, cheering you on and rooting for you because He loves you. He chose you. You are His.

God says He will never lose sight of you, never lose track of you, never let go of you. He will never forget you or forsake you or abandon you the way other people sometimes do.

No, He is here.

In this crazy world we live in, with all its chaos, all its change and uncertainty, He is our rock. He is our refuge, our shelter, our safe place. The storms of life may be raging all around us, but God holds us close.

Nothing can shake Him. Therefore nothing can shake us!

And nothing can tear us out of His hands (John 10:28).

The doors that God opens for us, no one can shut (Revelation 3:8).

His promises are unbreakable. His Word is 100 percent true.

"For no matter how many promises God has made, they are 'Yes' in Christ" (2 Corinthians 1:20 NIV).

We have so much to hope for, so much to believe in. Because God is here, and it's no secret what He can do!

think on it

When you think of a safe place, what do you imagine? How does it look or feel?

When the circumstances of life feel anything but safe, how can God still be your safe place?

Think of a hard season you've experienced. If you sought refuge in God, how did it feel to rest in Him as your safe space? If you didn't know God then, how do you think that season would've been different had you spent it with Him?

think on it

Psalm 145:18 says, "The Lord is close to all who call on him." How does it help to know that God is always nearby?

We don't always understand God. We don't always know what He's up to or what He will do. In Isaiah 55:8, God says, "I don't think the way you think. The way you work isn't the way I work" (The Message). Why is this a good thing? When do you most need to remember this scripture?

Psalm 145:17 says, "The Lord is righteous in all his ways and faithful in all he does" (NIV). Because He is God and because He is good, we know we can trust Him. Where do you see God's faithfulness in your life today? How does your answer reinforce the truth that hope is here?

Act on It

The psalmist exclaimed, "How good it is to be near God! I have made the Sovereign LORD my shelter, and I will tell everyone about the wonderful things you do" (Psalm 73:28).

Dream up the most beautiful, safe place you can think of. Picture yourself meeting God there right now, during your prayer time, as you share your heart with Him. In the space below, write down your prayer, asking God to sustain you with hope, no matter what comes your way. Keep coming back to this place in your mind whenever you need to remember God's protection and presence.

HIDE YOUR LOVED ONES IN THE SHELTER OF YOUR PRESENCE, SAFE BENEATH YOUR HAND.

PSALM 31:20 TLB

Day
11

Hope *in* God

Let your unfailing love surround us, Lord, for our hope is in you alone.

PSALM 33:22

The Lord is good to everyone. He showers compassion on all his creation.

PSALM 145:9

Psalm 145:13
NIV

The LORD is trustworthy in all he promises and faithful in all he does.

Luke 1:37

For the word of God will never fail.

Isaiah 12:2

The LORD GOD is my strength and my song; he has given me victory.

Psalm 18:2

The LORD is my rock, my fortress, and my savior; my God is my rock, in whom I find protection. He is my shield, the power that saves me.

Psalm 144:2

He is my loving ally and my fortress, my tower of safety, my rescuer. . . . I take refuge in him.

Psalm 34:5

Those who look to him for help will be radiant with joy.

Zephaniah 3:17
AMP

The LORD your God is in your midst, a Warrior who saves. He will rejoice over you with joy; He will be quiet in His love [making no mention of your past sins], He will rejoice over you with shouts of joy.

John 14:26
AMP

The Helper (Comforter, Advocate, Intercessor—Counselor, Strengthener, Standby), the Holy Spirit, whom the Father will send in My name [in My place, to represent Me and act on My behalf], He will teach you all things. And He will help you remember everything that I have told you.

Psalm 25:5
NIV

Guide me in your truth and teach me, for you are God my Savior, and my hope is in you all day long.

A NOTE FROM
Candace

Hope in God

Wild hope is hope in God. Hope in who He is. Hope in His promises. And because of who He is, God can be trusted to keep those promises. Absolutely each and every one.

Nothing can separate us from His love for us. That's what the Bible says:

> Neither death nor life, neither angels nor demons, neither our fears for today nor our worries about tomorrow—not even the powers of hell can separate us from God's love. No power in the sky above or in the earth below—indeed, nothing in all creation will ever be able to separate us from the love of God that is revealed in Christ Jesus our Lord. (Romans 8:38–39)

We can't even begin to imagine the height or width or depth of this great love. But we can trust it. We can stand on it. We can rest in it. And with God, nothing is impossible.

Nothing is too difficult for Him. Nothing is too hard, too long, too complicated, too overwhelming, too frustrating, or too messy. Nothing is beyond His strength, His skill, His power, His knowledge, or His wisdom and understanding.

Romans 11:33–36 exclaims,

> Have you ever come on anything quite like this extravagant generosity of God, this deep, deep wisdom? It's way over our heads. We'll never figure it out.
>
> Is there anyone around who can explain God?
> Anyone smart enough to tell him what to do?
> Anyone who has done him such a huge favor
> that God has to ask his advice?
> Everything comes from him;
> everything happens through him;
> everything ends up in him.
> Always glory! Always praise!
> Yes. Yes. Yes. (THE MESSAGE)

It's who God is. And that's our hope.

think on it

One of the ways Scripture teaches us to know God is to refer to Him by different names or descriptive titles. Take a look at a few from Scripture.

Creator	The Lord my provider	Prince of Peace
Lamb of God	Bread of Life	Righteous Judge
The God who sees me	Almighty God	The Lord of Heaven's Armies
The Vine	I Am	Living Water
Counselor	The Lord my banner/victory	Light of the world
Word of God	Savior	Hope of the world
The Lord my healer	Everlasting Father	God of hope
Good Shepherd	King of kings	Friend
Comforter	The Lord my righteousness	
God with us	Redeemer	

Write down the name you are most drawn to.

Reflect on what that name means to you. How have you experienced God this way? If you haven't, how or why do you long to?

Is there a name for God in the list you hadn't heard before? If so, how does that name renew your hope?

think on it

Take a look at some of the attributes or characteristics of God found in Scripture.

holy	all-knowing	glorious
faithful	righteous	wise
forgiving	compassionate	gracious
ever-present	humble	patient
just	all-powerful	unchanging
loving	merciful	sovereign
gentle	kind	

Write down the attribute that you connect with the most today.

How have you personally experienced this aspect of God's character?

How does knowing these names and characteristics of God make a difference in the challenges you face and the choices you make?

Act on It

Write a letter to God. Address Him by the name or title you chose on the previous pages. Take a few moments to praise Him for who He is and how He loves and cares for you. Then thank Him for what He has done, what He is doing, and what He will do.

O MY STRENGTH, TO YOU I SING PRAISES,
FOR YOU, O GOD, ARE MY REFUGE, THE GOD
WHO SHOWS ME UNFAILING LOVE.

PSALM 59:17

Day 12

Hope *in* His Word

I am counting on the Lord; yes, I am counting on him. I have put my hope in his word.

PSALM 130:5

There's nothing like the written Word of God for showing you the way to salvation through faith in Christ Jesus. Every part of Scripture is God-breathed and useful one way or another—showing us truth, exposing our rebellion, correcting our mistakes, training us to live God's way. Through the Word we are put together and shaped up for the tasks God has for us.

2 TIMOTHY 3:15–17 THE MESSAGE

Hebrews 4:12
AMP

For the word of God is living and active and full of power [making it operative, energizing, and effective].

1 Peter 1:23

Your new life will last forever because it comes from the eternal, living word of God.

Colossians 2:6–7

Now, just as you accepted Christ Jesus as your Lord, you must continue to follow him. Let your roots grow down into him, and let your lives be built on him. Then your faith will grow strong in the truth you were taught, and you will overflow with thankfulness.

Philippians 2:16

Hold firmly to the word of life.

Psalm 1:2–3
THE VOICE

For you, the Eternal's Word is your happiness. It is your focus—from dusk to dawn. You are like a tree, planted by *flowing, cool* streams of water *that never run dry*. Your fruit ripens in its time; your leaves never fade or curl *in the summer sun*. No matter what you do, you prosper.

A NOTE FROM *Candace*

Hope in His Word

Where do I find hope when life is hard? Where does my hope come from? My hope comes from the Lord! It really does.

When I'm discouraged or disappointed or frustrated, I know I can talk to my family. I can talk to my friends. And I know that—most of the time—they'll try to show their love and support. They'll try to speak encouraging words to me. But ultimately, my true hope and my real comfort come from God's Word.

No one knows me better than God does—and no one can be there for me like He can. No one can do what He can do. He alone has the power to work in my heart and life, to work miraculously in and through my circumstances for His glory and my good.

God alone has all the answers. He is the source of my comfort and strength. He is the One who sustains me. He has all the wisdom and direction I need, ready and waiting for me.

So I talk to Him. I pray. And I read my Bible to hear what He has to say.

I spend time in praise and worship, using words of Scripture to remind me who God is, what He has done for me, and why I can trust Him with everything.

I stand on His promises.

And I stay focused. I surround myself with people and things that will point me to His Word and remind me to put my hope in Him.

One of my go-to scriptures is Galatians 5:22–23: "The Holy Spirit produces this kind of fruit in our lives: love, joy, peace, patience, kindness, goodness, faithfulness, gentleness, and self-control."

Those words describe the attitude, character, and behavior I want to embody on a daily basis. I want to be a woman who is loving and joyful, good and faithful, patient and gentle and kind, and filled with peace. I want to be a woman of discipline and self-control.

When I'm struggling with any of these things, I go back to the Word of God and remind myself that I have the fruit of the Spirit. God's Spirit is living in me. I don't have to be anxious or cranky or stressed.

Through His Word and by His Spirit, I have help—all the help I need—to be the woman He created me to be.

think on it

In John 15:4–5, Jesus says, "Remain in me, and I will remain in you. For a branch cannot produce fruit if it is severed from the vine, and you cannot be fruitful unless you remain in me. Yes, I am the vine; you are the branches. Those who remain in me, and I in them, will produce much fruit." What's your favorite way to stay connected to Jesus? By praying, reading Scripture, worshiping Him in song, or something else?

How do you find time—or make time—to spend in God's Word?

What fruit has God's Word produced in your life?

think on it

As you think about consistently spending time in Bible reading and prayer, what are the biggest obstacles you face? What are your limitations or distractions? And what steps might you take to overcome them? (Don't forget to ask God to help you with this!)

How has God's Word given you hope or encouragement, strength or peace, wisdom or guidance? How does it shape the woman you are becoming?

The psalmist prayed, "Open my eyes to see the wonderful truths in your instructions" (Psalm 119:18). A few verses later, he added, "Revive and refresh me according to Your word" (v. 25 AMP). What are your go-to verses? Which scriptures revive, refresh, or refocus you time and time again? Think of a favorite and write it here.

Act on It

One of the best ways to find hope and help in God's Word is to memorize it. In Deuteronomy 6:6, God says, "Write these commandments that I've given you today on your hearts. Get them inside of you" (THE MESSAGE). When you have hidden God's Word in your heart, that scripture is there for you wherever you are, whenever you need it (Psalm 119:11).

Look back at the Bible verse you wrote down on the previous page. Now it's time to memorize it. Write the first word of the verse in the space provided. Now say the word aloud. Then write the first and second words. Say both aloud. Next, write the first three words and say all three aloud. Continue this pattern, adding one word at a time, and saying the full string of words aloud each time. Soon you'll have the verse hidden deep in your heart.

YOUR WORD IS MY SOURCE OF HOPE.

PSALM 119:114

Day
13

Hope *in* Prayer

I love the Lord because he hears my prayers and answers them.

PSALM 116:1 TLB

The first thing I want you to do is pray. Pray every way you know how, for everyone you know.

1 TIMOTHY 2:1 THE MESSAGE

Philippians 4:6	Don't worry about anything; instead, pray about everything. Tell God what you need, and thank him for all he has done.
Ephesians 6:18	Pray in the Spirit at all times and on every occasion. Stay alert and be persistent in your prayers for all believers everywhere.
Matthew 7:7–8	Keep on asking, and you will receive what you ask for. Keep on seeking, and you will find. Keep on knocking, and the door will be opened to you. For everyone who asks, receives. Everyone who seeks, finds. And to everyone who knocks, the door will be opened.
Romans 8:26–28 *THE MESSAGE*	The moment we get tired in the waiting, God's Spirit is right alongside helping us along. If we don't know how or what to pray, it doesn't matter. He does our praying in and for us, making prayer out of our wordless sighs, our aching groans. He knows us far better than we know ourselves . . . and keeps us present before God. That's why we can be so sure that every detail in our lives of love for God is worked into something good.
Colossians 4:2 *AMP*	Be persistent and devoted to prayer, being alert and focused in your prayer life with an attitude of thanksgiving.
1 Thessalonians 5:16–18	Always be joyful. Never stop praying. Be thankful in all circumstances, for this is God's will for you who belong to Christ Jesus.

A NOTE FROM *Candace*

Hope in Prayer

Wild hope—biblical hope—isn't daydreaming or wishful thinking or anxious hand-wringing. It isn't complacent or passive or powerless. It does involve waiting, though, because we can only hope for something we don't yet have or something that hasn't yet happened.

But this kind of waiting is an active waiting. Waiting with energy and expectation. With anticipation.

A disciplined and diligent waiting. A purposeful waiting.

A prayerful waiting.

You know, praying isn't the only thing we can do while we wait, but it's the absolute best thing! Rather than a last resort—what we turn to when all else fails—prayer should be the very first thing we do, the foundation of any effort we make.

The possibilities of prayer are some of the biggest reasons we have hope to begin with. We have hope because we know we can talk to God about everything that concerns us. We know He hears us and that He answers our prayers. We know our prayers make a difference. They matter. God says so—over and over in His Word.

So as we wait in hope, we pray—about everyone and everything on our hearts, about every circumstance we find ourselves in, and about every challenge or opportunity we face.

Pray purposefully, actively, deliberately, constantly. Pause during your day for special times of focused prayer and for spontaneous moments of prayer. The Bible calls this prayer "without ceasing" (1 Thessalonians 5:17 KJV). Keep a running conversation with God—both talking and listening.

To me there's such hope in realizing that we don't need to have all the answers to life's questions. We don't have to figure things out on our own. God has the answers for us. He has the power, the wisdom, the strength, and the grace that we simply don't—and He wants to give it to us! All we have to do is ask.

And even there, He helps us. God knows we don't always have the right words. We don't always know what to say or how to pray. So He translates our longings, our hopes and dreams, our deepest needs, and our thoughts and feelings into prayers. And He loves to answer our prayers.

think on it

How would you describe your prayer life right now?

What form do your prayers take? When, where, how often, and for how long do you pray?

What prompts you to pray?

think on it

How do you experience God's presence in prayer? Are you aware of Him being there? In your experience, how does He answer prayer?

How would you like to grow in your prayer life? Would you like to try any prayer practices or traditions that others find helpful? What are some other steps you could take to grow your prayer life?

The psalmist said, "I took my troubles to the Lord; I cried out to him, and he answered my prayer" (Psalm 120:1). What is troubling you right now? What are your prayer requests today? Jot them down here and take some time right now to pray, in the hope and faith that God will hear and answer.

Act on It

Sometimes we get so busy or distracted as we go about our day that we forget to pray. Or we find ourselves stressing or strategizing instead of praying. But we can form better habits when we are intentional and make plans to pray.

Here's something simple you can do today. Choose a visual prompt, something you might see from time to time throughout the day, like a blue car on the highway or a bird in the sky. Then, decide who or what you will pray for whenever you see that visual cue. Write down five visual prompts and what you will pray for when you see them.

AS SOON AS I PRAY, YOU ANSWER ME; YOU ENCOURAGE ME BY GIVING ME STRENGTH.

PSALM 138:3

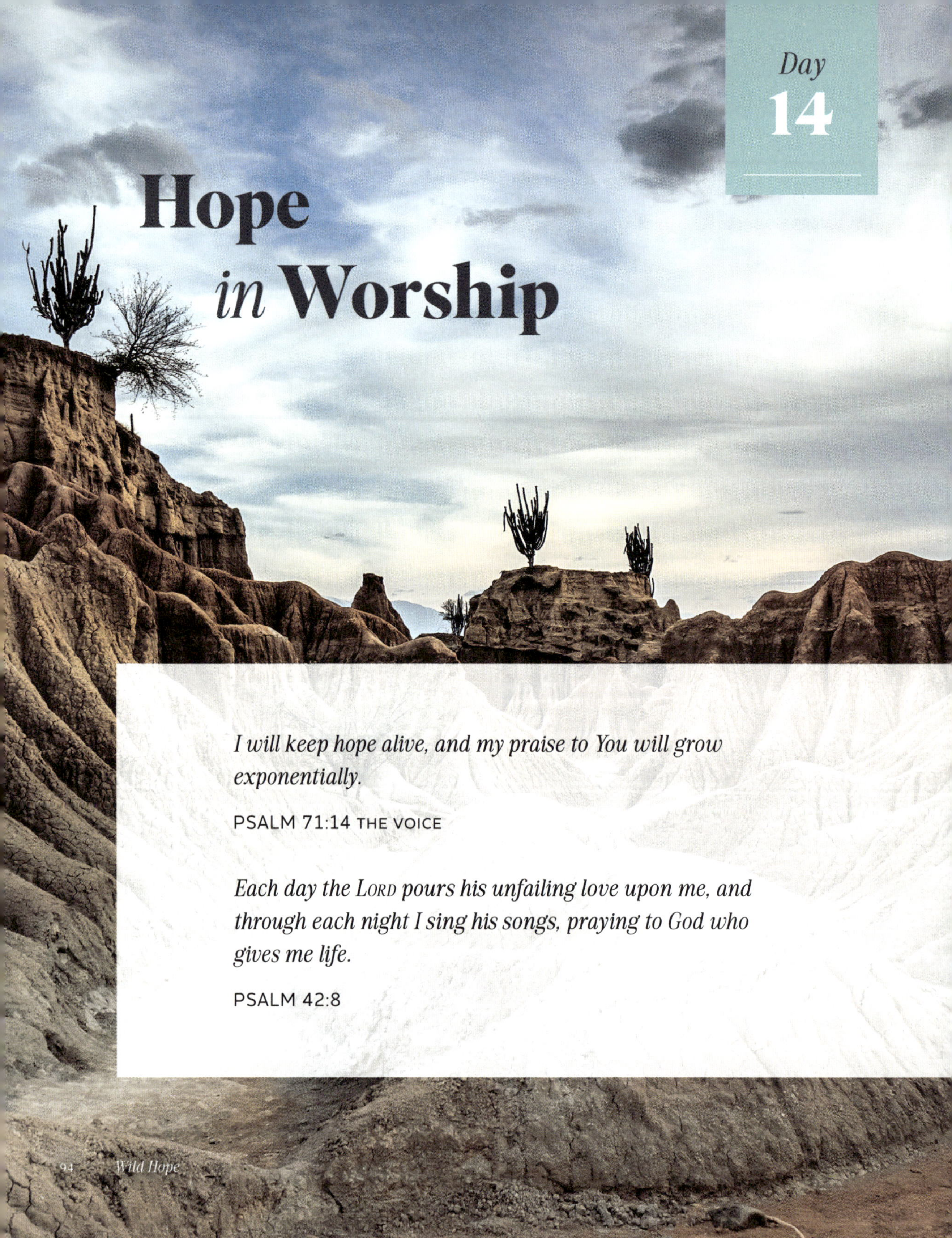

Day
14

Hope *in* Worship

I will keep hope alive, and my praise to You will grow exponentially.

PSALM 71:14 THE VOICE

Each day the Lord pours his unfailing love upon me, and through each night I sing his songs, praying to God who gives me life.

PSALM 42:8

Psalm 103:1–2
THE VOICE

O my soul, *come*, praise the Eternal with all that is in me—*body, emotions, mind, and will—every part of who I am*—praise His holy name. O my soul, *come*, praise the Eternal; *sing a song from a grateful heart; sing and* never forget all the good He has done.

Psalm 28:7

The LORD is my strength and shield. I trust him with all my heart. He helps me, and my heart is filled with joy. I burst out in songs of thanksgiving.

Psalm 89:15

Happy are those who hear the joyful call to worship, for they will walk in the light of your presence, LORD.

Psalm 105:1–5
THE MESSAGE

Hallelujah! Thank GOD! Pray to him by name! Tell everyone you meet what he has done! Sing him songs, belt out hymns, translate his wonders into music! Honor his holy name with Hallelujahs, you who seek GOD. Live a happy life! Keep your eyes open for GOD, watch for his works; be alert for signs of his presence. Remember the world of wonders he has made.

Ephesians 5:18–20

Be filled with the Holy Spirit, singing psalms and hymns and spiritual songs among yourselves, and making music to the Lord in your hearts. And give thanks for everything to God the Father in the name of our Lord Jesus Christ.

1 Peter 3:15

Worship Christ as Lord of your life. And if someone asks about your hope as a believer, always be ready to explain it.

A NOTE FROM *Candace*

Hope in Worship

The Bible tells us that generations of God's people have found hope—and help—in worship. Whether they were anxious or afraid, racked with grief and pain, lost or lonely or confused, or under attack physically or spiritually, they worshiped. They lifted their eyes, their hearts, their hands, and their voices to God in prayer and praise. The more they remembered who God is and what He had done for them in the past, the more they were encouraged in their faith in the present and the more they were filled with hope for the future.

Of course, God's people gave thanks and praise beyond the tough times. Worship was a big part of every celebration, every feast day or holiday, and every special occasion. Because worship was—and is—for every day. God said, "I will give them one heart and one purpose: to worship me forever, for their own good and for the good of all their descendants" (Jeremiah 32:39).

Yes, we were made to worship. And when we do, we experience God's presence in a very special way. We find a hope and help we can't get any other way.

We worship God with our words (spoken, written, or sung). We worship Him with our hearts and minds and spirits. We worship Him with our bodies. We worship Him with our lives. We worship Him with our attitudes and our actions—the choices we make each day.

Each of these things can be a form of worship, an expression of our trust in God, a declaration of our love for and gratitude to Him.

Each one draws us closer to Him and toward a hope-filled, joy-filled life of faith.

think on it

How do you worship God in the good times, the bad times, and the in-between times? Do you plan celebrations with God? Do you journal your prayers during dark times? What practical steps do you take to make worship a part of your life?

Who has a practice of worship that inspires you? Feel free to name a person in your own life or an example from the Bible. How does this person model worship?

What can you do to improve your personal worship—the time you set apart to seek God and affirm who He is?

think on it

How do your daily actions reflect a heart of worship? Which of your actions do not reflect a heart of worship?

Do you see worship as a source of strength or as a religious obligation? Why?

How does worship renew your hope in God? How does it change your attitude and outlook?

Act on It

The Bible has a lot to say about worship—I mean, *a lot*! It includes all kinds of stories and examples of worship, but many of us will first think of the book of Psalms. In essence, Psalms is a treasury of the world's greatest worship songs, and God's people have sung—and continue to sing—them in dozens of languages, in hundreds of countries, for thousands of years. These same songs, these same psalms, have also inspired thousands of new songs.

Today you're going to write a psalm of your own! If you need inspiration, flip through your Bible or look over some of the many psalms quoted in these pages.

Follow these instructions and write your answers in a notebook:

1. Speak directly to God. Write His name—God, Lord, Jesus, Father, or whichever name feels natural to you. (See page 79 for a reminder of some of God's names.)
2. Tell God how you're feeling today, good or bad.
3. Affirm who God is and what you love about Him.
4. Describe what God has done for you in the past—your personal evidence of His faithfulness, mercy, and love.
5. Thank God for what He will do in the future—how He will care for you, lead you and guide you, protect you, and provide for you.
6. End with a declaration of your continued faith and trust in Him.

If you want to, you can copy your psalm into your journal, post it online, set it to music, or scrapbook it!

SING PSALMS AND HYMNS AND SPIRITUAL SONGS TO GOD WITH THANKFUL HEARTS.

COLOSSIANS 3:16

Day
15

Hope *in the* Ordinary

He has made everything beautiful in its time.

ECCLESIASTES 3:11 NIV

God, the Lord, created the heavens and stretched them out. He created the earth and everything in it. He gives breath to everyone, life to everyone who walks the earth.

ISAIAH 42:5

Colossians 1:17	He existed before anything else, and he holds all creation together.
Psalm 19:1	The heavens proclaim the glory of God. The skies display his craftsmanship.
Psalm 95:4–5	He holds in his hands the depths of the earth and the mightiest mountains. The sea belongs to him, for he made it. His hands formed the dry land, too.
Psalm 104:24–25	O LORD, what a variety of things you have made! In wisdom you have made them all. The earth is full of your creatures. Here is the ocean, vast and wide, teeming with life of every kind, both large and small.
Psalm 74:17 THE VOICE	You have arranged the earth, set all its boundaries; You are the Architect of *the seasons*: summer and winter.
Psalm 8:3–4	When I look at the night sky and see the work of your fingers—the moon and the stars you set in place—what are mere mortals that you should think about them, human beings that you should care for them?
Psalm 139:14 AMP	I will give thanks and praise to You, for I am fearfully and wonderfully made; wonderful are Your works, and my soul knows it very well.
Ephesians 2:10	We are God's masterpiece. He has created us anew in Christ Jesus, so we can do the good things he planned for us long ago.

A NOTE FROM *Candace*

Hope in the Ordinary

The world is full of ordinary, everyday miracles—the kind of miracles that are easy to miss, easy to take for granted. You've probably experienced miracles like these recently:

- The beauty and majesty and magnificence of creation—this wonderful world God made and all who live in it!
- The daily faithfulness of so many good people who care for their families and their communities without fanfare or applause, who live unselfishly, lovingly, generously, and courageously through all of life's ups and downs.
- The random acts of kindness one stranger does for another.

On the most ordinary days and in the most ordinary seasons, we can find evidence of God's extraordinary love for us. His guidance. His protection and provision. His tender mercy. His favor and blessing. John 1:16 explains, "For out of His fullness [the super-abundance of His grace and truth] we have all received grace upon grace [spiritual blessing upon spiritual blessing, favor upon favor, and gift heaped upon gift]" (AMP).

Gift after gift. God has already given us gifts, and He continues to give them. We just have to learn to look for them.

When we do, we'll find more than we can count. We'll find all kinds of gifts that give us hope and encouragement in good times and in bad, in exciting and extraordinary seasons, and in the ordinary and the everyday.

So how can we show our gratitude to God for these gifts? Romans 12:1 says, "So here's what I want you to do, God helping you: Take your everyday, ordinary life—your sleeping, eating, going-to-work, and walking-around life—and place it before God as an offering" (THE MESSAGE).

Thank God for ordinary miracles. Be encouraged by everyday blessings. And point them out to those around you! These gifts from God stir up hope in all of us.

think on it

Read how Ecclesiastes 3:1–8 metaphorically describes some of the different seasons of life.

For everything there is a season,
a time for every activity under heaven.
A time to be born and a time to die.
A time to plant and a time to harvest.
A time to kill and a time to heal.
A time to tear down and a time to build up.
A time to cry and a time to laugh.
A time to grieve and a time to dance.
A time to scatter stones and a time to gather stones.
A time to embrace and a time to turn away.
A time to search and a time to quit searching.
A time to keep and a time to throw away.
A time to tear and a time to mend.
A time to be quiet and a time to speak.
A time to love and a time to hate.
A time for war and a time for peace.

Which of these seasons of life are you in right now?

What ordinary, everyday miracles have you seen lately?

What have you learned in this season that will help you find hope in the next season?

think on it

Would you say this is an *ordinary* or *extraordinary* time for you? What do you think God is leading you toward?

God gives us gift after gift after gift. And in return, He wants us to give Him our lives. What part of your life have you not yet given to God? How can you give it to God today?

How can you share ordinary, everyday miracles with others in your life?

Act on It

What seemingly ordinary thing could you do to bring someone else a burst of hope?

Could you send a card, a note, or a text? Could you stop by for a visit or invite someone over? Could you drop off some flowers, bake some brownies, help out with a project, or run an errand? Could you donate something, offer to babysit, or volunteer? Could you share a friendly smile, hold open a door, give up a parking space, help someone with luggage, or let someone cut ahead of you in line?

Brainstorm some doable actions and write them below. And then do them! Don't forget to tell God you're willing and available for His use—and keep your eyes open for any spontaneous or sudden opportunities He sends you.

WHENEVER WE HAVE THE OPPORTUNITY, WE SHOULD DO GOOD TO EVERYONE.

GALATIANS 6:10

Day

16

Hope *in the* Extraordinary

To have faith is to be sure of the things we hope for, to be certain of the things we cannot see.

HEBREWS 11:1 GNT

We stand surrounded by all those who have gone before, *an enormous cloud of witnesses.*

HEBREWS 12:1 THE VOICE

Hebrews 11:33–35

By faith these people overthrew kingdoms, ruled with justice, and received what God had promised them. They shut the mouths of lions, quenched the flames of fire, and escaped death by the edge of the sword. Their weakness was turned to strength. They became strong in battle and put whole armies to flight. . . . But others were tortured, refusing to turn from God in order to be set free. They placed their hope in a better life after the resurrection.

Philippians 1:23–25

I'm torn between two desires: I long to go and be with Christ, which would be far better for me. But for your sakes, it is better that I continue to live. Knowing this, I am convinced that I will remain alive so I can continue to help all of you grow and experience the joy of your faith.

Philippians 4:1
NIV

Therefore, my brothers and sisters, you whom I love and long for, my joy and crown, stand firm in the Lord in this way, dear friends!

Hebrews 12:2
AMP

Focusing our eyes on Jesus, who is the Author and Perfecter of faith . . . who for the joy [of accomplishing the goal] set before Him endured the cross.

Ephesians 3:20–21
AMP

Now to Him who is able to [carry out His purpose and] do superabundantly more than all that we dare ask or think [infinitely beyond our greatest prayers, hopes, or dreams], according to His power that is at work within us, to Him be the glory in the church and in Christ Jesus throughout all generations forever and ever. Amen.

Hope in the Extraordinary

Sometimes hope looks extraordinary. And we find it in some pretty extraordinary stories.

I'm thinking of the story of Hollywood producer Jonathan Koch, who has been a mentor and friend to me since I was twelve years old. While attending a conference in 2015, Jonathan became desperately ill. Doctors had to put him in a coma in order to save his life. He ended up losing all or part of all four limbs, including all of his right foot and left hand.

Surgery after surgery followed, and then an incredibly difficult journey to recovery. Jonathan said it was so intense, he felt like he was in hell. But he didn't want to leave his daughter without a father. And he didn't want to leave Jennifer, the woman who had just become his wife.

So he kept talking to God through his pain. He kept fighting to survive, day after day after day. Against all odds, he found hope. And he kept finding it, kept fighting for it.

Eventually, he made history as the recipient of a first-of-its-kind experimental hand transplant. His doctors thought it would take him years to get used to it, but Jonathan was on the tennis courts using his new hand in just four months. With his wife and daughter, he rebuilt his life, and eventually he returned to work as a busy film producer. Now he travels all over the world telling his story and helping others find hope.

I know his story does that for me. It gives me hope.

And Jonathan's story isn't the only one. There are many amazing stories like his, stories that remind us that people can and do find ways—against all odds—to overcome all kinds of hardship, suffering, and pain. To triumph over adversity. To live with extraordinary hope, courage, strength, and grace to the very end.

The point is not to compare our stories to theirs but to take their stories to heart.

If we keep talking to God, keep fighting the good fight, keep holding on to our wild hope, we *can* find joy and victory—no matter what we face.

think on it

How has your hope—and your faith—been tested in your life? What moment or situation has pushed you to your limit?

Psalm 66:8–12 says, "Bless our God, O peoples! Give him a thunderous welcome! Didn't he set us on the road to life? Didn't he keep us out of the ditch? He trained us first, passed us like silver through refining fires, brought us into hardscrabble country, pushed us to our very limit, road-tested us inside and out, took us to hell and back; finally he brought us to this well-watered place" (THE MESSAGE). Can you relate to these verses? How has God trained you for tough seasons?

Are you in a place of training or testing, or in a season of rest and refreshing?

think on it

When have you, against all odds, held on to hope?

Romans 8:18 reminds us that no matter how a situation feels, "what we suffer now is nothing compared to the glory [God] will reveal to us later"—the reward, the blessing He has in store. And nothing is wasted. Romans 8:28 says, "God causes everything to work together for the good of those who love God and are called according to his purpose for them." How have you experienced this? What hope do these words give you right now?

Second Corinthians 1:3–4 says, "God is our merciful Father and the source of all comfort. He comforts us in all our troubles so that we can comfort others. When they are troubled, we will be able to give them the same comfort God has given us." When have you been able to help someone else because of what you've experienced? If you haven't yet, how could you help someone who's gone through a hardship similar to yours?

Act on It

Sometimes we talk about "finding our why." Our why is what motivates and inspires us. It gives us a sense of purpose, focus, and determination. It gives our actions meaning. And our why helps us dig deep and find the courage we need to overcome the challenges we face.

In the space below, write your why for taking on or facing an extraordinary challenge. Your why may be your life's mission, a big-picture goal, or a dream. Let your why remind you of the hope we have in God.

HE WILL KEEP YOU STRONG TO THE END.

1 CORINTHIANS 1:8

Day
17

Hope *from the* Past

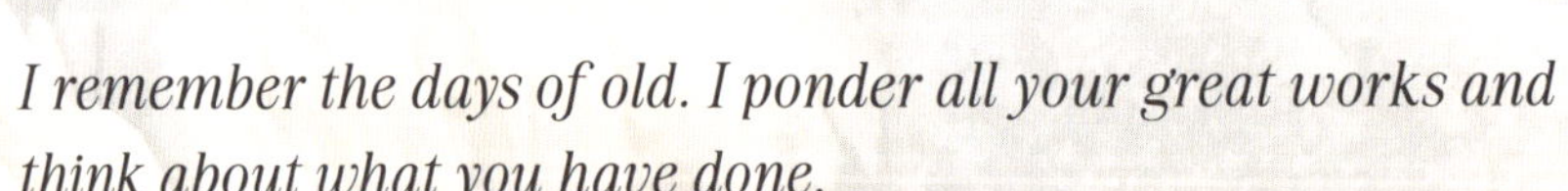

I remember the days of old. I ponder all your great works and think about what you have done.

PSALM 143:5

Surely you are still our Father! . . . You are our Redeemer from ages past.

ISAIAH 63:16

Psalm 90:1–2 AMP

Lord, You have been our dwelling place [our refuge, our sanctuary, our stability] in all generations. Before the mountains were born or before You had given birth to the earth and the world, even from everlasting to everlasting, You are [the eternal] God.

Psalm 77:11–12

I recall all you have done, O LORD; I remember your wonderful deeds of long ago. They are constantly in my thoughts. I cannot stop thinking about your mighty works.

Psalm 65:5

You faithfully answer our prayers with awesome deeds, O God our savior. You are the hope of everyone on earth.

Romans 15:4

Such things were written in the Scriptures long ago to teach us. And the Scriptures give us hope and encouragement as we wait patiently for God's promises to be fulfilled.

Psalm 25:6

Remember, O LORD, your compassion and unfailing love, which you have shown from long ages past.

Psalm 71:17–18

O God, you have taught me from my earliest childhood, and I constantly tell others about the wonderful things you do. Now that I am old and gray, do not abandon me, O God. Let me proclaim your power to this new generation, your mighty miracles to all who come after me.

Hebrews 10:23

Let us hold tightly without wavering to the hope we affirm, for God can be trusted to keep his promise.

A NOTE FROM *Candace*

Hope from the Past

The Bible tells us that when Joshua led God's people into the promised land, God did many amazing things to show His people that He was with them. God had been with them when He miraculously delivered them from slavery and oppression in Egypt (and before that!). And He hadn't abandoned them as they wandered in the wilderness in stubbornness and rebellion for forty years.

No, God was still with them, every day. Every step of the way.

He still loved them. He still had a plan and a purpose for them.

He promised to bless them in the new land He was giving them (Deuteronomy 28).

God knew His people would go through some hard times. It wouldn't be easy making a new home in this new place. But they weren't going to face these challenges alone. They would *never* be alone. And He reminded them of this in a pretty spectacular way. (See Joshua 3–4 for the full story.)

When God's people arrived at the banks of the Jordan River, the river was at its fullest. God told them to cross it anyway. Suddenly, just as their leaders stepped into the water at the river's edge, that running river came to a complete standstill!

The water backed up at a town "a great distance away," and the people walked across on dry land (Joshua 3:16). Then, once everyone had made it safely to the other side, Joshua sent the leaders back to the riverbed to gather large stones.

Joshua said, "We will use these stones to build a memorial. In the future your children will ask you, 'What do these stones mean?' Then you can tell them. . . . These stones will stand as a memorial among the people of Israel forever" (4:6–7).

I just love this! It's so important to remember how God has been with us in the past—how He has rescued us, protected us, and provided for us. How He has answered our prayers.

And it's not just important to remember; it's also important to share these truths with others—to keep the stories alive by telling them to our children and grandchildren.

It's one of the best ways I know of to hold on to hope—and pass that hope on to future generations!

think on it

The Bible is filled with stories of men and women who put their hope, faith, and trust in God. Their stories are there to remind us of God's love and care. What are some of your favorites?

Think of other stories of men and women (in history, perhaps) who—by God's grace—have persevered in extraordinary circumstances, overcome incredible odds, or accomplished amazing things. What have these stories inspired you to do in your life?

Do you know people who have lived quiet lives of everyday faithfulness? How do their examples give you hope as you make your own way through life?

think on it

When has God created a clear path for you to take?

In Malachi 3:6, God says, "I am the Lord, and I do not change." And Hebrews 13:8 tells us "Jesus Christ is the same yesterday, today, and forever." What characteristic of God that you've seen in the past gives you hope for your circumstances today?

Psalm 103:1–2 says, "Let all that I am praise the Lord; with my whole heart, I will praise his holy name. Let all that I am praise the Lord; may I never forget the good things he does for me." Take a few moments to list some of the good things God has done and praise Him for them.

Act on It

Just as Joshua built a stone memorial next to the Jordan River, you can create your own type of memorial to help you remember what God has done *for* you, *in* you, and *through* you. For instance, you could keep a journal or a scrapbook of special moments. You could use your social media to share what God has done, knowing that in the future the posts will pop up in your feed as "memories"! You could collect specific objects (such as charms on a bracelet) that symbolize your stories. Or if Joshua's example resonates with you, consider collecting small stones in a vase or bowl and using a marker to write meaningful words or important dates on them to remind you of what God has done.

What will you do? Write your plan below. Whatever you choose, share your idea with your family and friends so you never forget what God has done for you!

KEEP YOUR EYES OPEN FOR GOD, WATCH FOR HIS WORKS; BE ALERT FOR SIGNS OF HIS PRESENCE. REMEMBER THE WORLD OF WONDERS HE HAS MADE, HIS MIRACLES.

PSALM 105:4–5 THE MESSAGE

Day
18

Hope *in the* Present

Now I can walk in your presence, O God, in your life-giving light.

PSALM 56:13

Make sure that you don't get so absorbed and exhausted in taking care of all your day-by-day obligations that you lose track of the time and doze off, oblivious to God. The night is about over, dawn is about to break. Be up and awake to what God is doing! God is putting the finishing touches on the salvation work he began when we first believed. We can't afford to waste a minute, must not squander these precious daylight hours in frivolity and indulgence, in sleeping around and dissipation, in bickering and grabbing everything in sight. Get out of bed and get dressed! Don't loiter and linger, waiting until the very last minute. Dress yourselves in Christ, and be up and about!

ROMANS 13:11–14 THE MESSAGE

Hebrews 3:12–13
AMP

Encourage one another every day, as long as it is called Today."

2 Corinthians 6:1–10
THE MESSAGE

Companions as we are in this work with you, we beg you, please don't squander one bit of this marvelous life God has given us. God reminds us, "I heard your call in the nick of time; the day you needed me, I was there to help." Well, now is the right time to listen, the day to be helped. Don't put it off; don't frustrate God's work by showing up late, throwing a question mark over everything we're doing. Our work as God's servants gets validated—or not—in the details. People are watching us as we stay at our post, alertly, unswervingly . . . in hard times, tough times, bad times; when we're beaten up, jailed, and mobbed; working hard, working late, working without eating; with pure heart, clear head, steady hand; in gentleness, holiness, and honest love; when we're telling the truth, and when God's showing his power; when we're doing our best setting things right; when we're praised, and when we're blamed; slandered, and honored; true to our word, though distrusted; ignored by the world, but recognized by God; terrifically alive, though rumored to be dead; beaten within an inch of our lives, but refusing to die; immersed in tears, yet always filled with deep joy; living on handouts, yet enriching many; having nothing, having it all.

A NOTE FROM
Candace

Hope in the Present

Today—the one we're in right now—is a day to live in wild hope. Because "this is the day the LORD has made. We will rejoice and be glad in it" (Psalm 118:24). No matter what happens, no matter what obstacles or challenges we face, we know God is with us. He is in control. And this day is full of possibilities, full of opportunities, full of blessings—some in disguise!

In one sense, this is the only day we really have. Tomorrow isn't promised to any of us (Proverbs 27:1).

I don't know about you, but I don't want to miss a moment of this day. I don't want to sleepwalk through it—numb or unfocused or distracted. I don't want to spend it procrastinating—putting off the things that are truly important, meaningful, or significant. I don't want to spend it living in the past or worrying about the future.

Ephesians 5:16 urges us to make "the very most of your time [on earth, recognizing and taking advantage of each opportunity and using it with wisdom and diligence]" (AMP).

And that's how I want to live.

I want to make the most of this day.

I want to work hard, do good, be kind, and love well.

I want to bring glory and honor to God.

I want to listen for His voice, pay attention to His presence, and follow His lead.

I *know* He is up to something good—in your life and in mine. And I don't want to miss a minute of it!

So here's what I'm praying:

Lord, give us all eyes to see, ears to hear, and hearts to respond to what You are doing in us and in the world today.

think on it

Matthew 6:34 says, "Give your entire attention to what God is doing right now, and don't get worked up about what may or may not happen tomorrow. God will help you deal with whatever hard things come up when the time comes" (THE MESSAGE). So what is God doing in your life right now?

What challenges, responsibilities, or opportunities do you need to focus on today? Which relationships are you prioritizing? How can you give the important things your entire attention?

What things can you let go of—the things that may or may not happen—and choose not to get "worked up" over today? As you jot them down, imagine putting them in God's hands, one by one, and asking Him to carry them for you.

think on it

Are you "sleepwalking" or putting off something important? How is that impacting you? How would your day—and your life—look different if you decided to truly engage in the day God has given you?

Colossians 3:23 says, "Work willingly at whatever you do, as though you were working for the Lord rather than for people." How can choosing this attitude help you today? What difference will it make in what you accomplish?

"This is why we work hard and continue to struggle, for our hope is in the living God, who is the Savior of all people and particularly of all believers" (1 Timothy 4:10). How would you describe the relationship between hard work and wild hope?

Act on It

Maybe you've heard this expression: "Yesterday is history. Tomorrow is a mystery. Today is a gift. That's why it is called 'the present.'"

In the space below, I invite you to journal and imagine this day, today, as a gift from God. Think about the blessings present in this day. Imagine a few surprises God might send your way. Then pray and ask God to help you receive this day as a gift. Ask Him to help you live with wild hope. Then ask Him to help you stay present and mindful as you go about your day, making the most of it!

And when this day—this gift—comes to an end, come back and note what was wrapped up inside. Give thanks to God for all you have received from Him.

THANKS BE TO GOD FOR HIS INDESCRIBABLE GIFT!

2 CORINTHIANS 9:15 NIV

Day
19

Hope *for the* Future

God can do anything, you know—far more than you could ever imagine or guess or request in your wildest dreams!

EPHESIANS 3:20 THE MESSAGE

"For I know the plans I have for you," declares the LORD, "plans to prosper you and not to harm you, plans to give you hope and a future."

JEREMIAH 29:11 NIV

Isaiah 43:19	I am about to do something new. See, I have already begun! Do you not see it? I will make a pathway through the wilderness. I will create rivers in the dry wasteland.
Revelation 21:5	Look, I am making everything new!
Psalm 40:5 NIV	Many, LORD my God, are the wonders you have done, the things you planned for us. None can compare with you; were I to speak and tell of your deeds, they would be too many to declare.
Psalm 139:1–5	O LORD, you have examined my heart and know everything about me. You know when I sit down or stand up. You know my thoughts even when I'm far away. You see me when I travel and when I rest at home. You know everything I do. You know what I am going to say even before I say it, LORD. You go before me and follow me. You place your hand of blessing on my head.
Psalm 139:16	You saw me before I was born. Every day of my life was recorded in your book. Every moment was laid out before a single day had passed.
Psalm 138:8	The LORD will work out his plans for my life—for your faithful love, O LORD, endures forever.

A NOTE FROM *Candace*

Hope for the Future

I live in wild hope—hope that motivates me, energizes me, and empowers me to dream big and work hard to accomplish all kinds of "impossible" things.

And although I try to be present—to live in the moment—I also live in the future. I'm always looking ahead to the next dream, the next goal, the next project or plan, or the next season of life. The next adventure!

Whether I'm considering new career opportunities, brainstorming business ideas, imagining becoming a grandparent one day, or longing for and looking forward to heaven and eternity, I'm genuinely excited about *whatever* comes next because I know God has good things in store for me—just as He does for you.

He created us with a plan and a purpose in mind—a calling. He's given us all kinds of strengths, gifts, and talents He wants us to explore. He's taught us so many things and wants us to apply them to our own lives and pass those lessons on to others.

The opportunities and the possibilities are endless!

I don't think I'm being unrealistic here. I've faced my share of dark days and tough times, and I know you have too. You may even be walking through one of those tough times as we speak. But as the saying goes, "Tough times never last. Tough people do!"

God uses tough times to make us strong and resilient. We come out on the other side with all kinds of treasures. Just as God intended.

Nothing we face is a surprise to Him. Nothing catches Him off guard or unprepared. Whatever it is—and I mean *whatever*—God's got this! And because He does, we do too!

This is the hope I'm talking about, the hope that gets me bouncing out of bed in the morning (most of the time!), eager to take on a new day. I can't wait to see what good things God has planned and what blessings He has in store.

Our future is absolutely and amazingly bright—because of Him.

think on it

Proverbs 31:30–31 describes a strong woman—a woman of virtue, a woman of valor—this way: "Charm *can* be deceptive and *physical* beauty will not last, but a woman who reveres the Eternal should be praised *above all others*. Celebrate all she has achieved. Let all her accomplishments publicly praise her" (THE VOICE). What are some significant or meaningful things God has already helped you accomplish? What has He given you the strength and the skill to achieve?

Further describing the Proverbs 31 woman, Scripture says, "Clothed in strength and dignity, *with nothing to fear*, she smiles *when she thinks* about the future" (v. 25 THE VOICE). What makes *you* smile when you think about the future? What are you looking forward to? What hopes and dreams do you have for the days to come?

Ephesians 1:11 tells us that God "makes everything work out according to his plan." How have you experienced this in your own life? Was it just as you hoped and dreamed?

think on it

Have God's plans unfolded in ways you didn't expect? How did you feel about that at the time?

What blessings have come out of hard or unexpected times?

Proverbs 16:9 reminds us, "We can make our plans, but the LORD determines our steps." Write a prayer, committing your current plans to God: your to-do list, your goals, your hopes, and your dreams. Ask Him to guide you every step of the way—and if necessary, redirect you according to what He knows is best.

Act on It

We can say with every confidence that our future is bright because our future is in God's hands. This is what fills us with wild hope!

Imagine that you're opening a time capsule from your *future* self who is ten years ahead of you. There are two or three items inside that represent God's faithfulness in your life. In the space below, list what those items are. How do they symbolize your bold hope in God for your future? How can they prepare you for your future? Then take one small step today in the direction of hope. It may be making an appointment, having a conversation, praying intentionally, or doing something else that leads you toward a wild hope in God for your future.

YOU HAVE BEEN CALLED TO ONE GLORIOUS HOPE FOR THE FUTURE.

EPHESIANS 4:4

Day
20

Hope Abounds

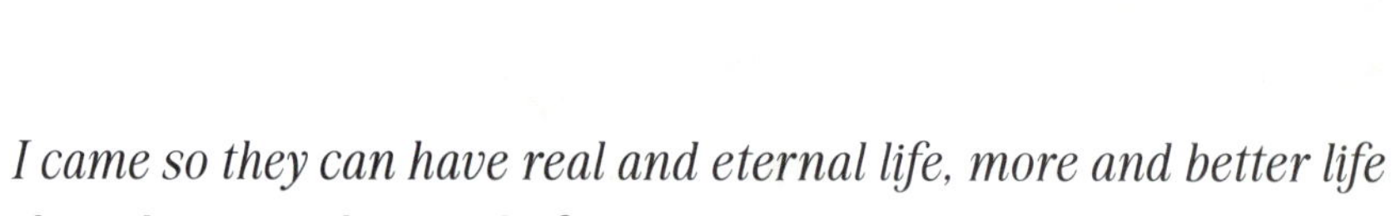

I came so they can have real and eternal life, more and better life than they ever dreamed of.

JOHN 10:10 THE MESSAGE

May the God of hope fill you with all joy and peace in believing [through the experience of your faith] that by the power of the Holy Spirit you will abound in hope and overflow with confidence in His promises.

ROMANS 15:13 AMP

Philippians 4:19–20
THE MESSAGE

You can be sure that God will take care of everything you need, his generosity exceeding even yours in the glory that pours from Jesus. Our God and Father abounds in glory that just pours out into eternity. Yes.

2 Corinthians 9:8
NIV

God is able to bless you abundantly, so that in all things at all times, having all that you need, you will abound in every good work.

Hebrews 4:16
AMP

Therefore let us [with privilege] approach the throne of grace [that is, the throne of God's gracious favor] with confidence and without fear, so that we may receive mercy [for our failures] and find [His amazing] grace to help in time of need [an appropriate blessing, coming just at the right moment].

1 Thessalonians 3:11–13
THE MESSAGE

May God our Father himself and our Master Jesus clear the road to you! And may the Master pour on the love so it fills your lives and splashes over on everyone around you, just as it does from us to you. May you be infused with strength and purity, filled with confidence in the presence of God our Father when our Master Jesus arrives with all his followers.

Hope Abounds

Some days are harder than others, but even on our hardest days, we are not without hope. We are never without hope. We are never without Jesus.

And Jesus reminds us that the life He has called us to is a good life, a rich and full life. A beautiful life—even with its heartache and pain.

Hope helps us see the good life. Hope helps us feel it and believe it. And this hope abounds! It's everywhere, all around us.

Hope says our story isn't finished yet. "So be truly glad," the apostle Peter wrote. "There is wonderful joy ahead" (1 Peter 1:6). Miracles are still coming, and answers to prayer are already on the way.

"So I tell you," Jesus said, "keep on asking, and you will receive what you ask for. Keep on seeking, and you will find. Keep on knocking, and the door will be opened to you" (Luke 11:9).

My mom is such a great example of someone who kept asking. Many years ago, during a crisis in her marriage, she came to faith in Christ and started taking us kids to church with her. But my dad wasn't interested.

Mom found all kinds of hope and joy in her faith. She was growing spiritually by leaps and bounds. It made her a much happier wife and a much happier mother.

But still, my dad said, "No, thanks. It's not for me." For thirty-five years, that was his answer.

Mom was full of hope anyway (though I'm sure she had some tough days). And being full of hope, she kept believing, kept trusting, and kept praying that one day my dad would find this hope too—that he would find faith. And one day, he did. Today he even teaches Bible studies and volunteers in prison ministry.

When hope abounds, it changes everything.

think on it

Proverbs 13:12 says, "Hope postponed grieves the heart; but when a dream comes true, life is full *and sweet*" (The Voice). How have you experienced this? Which hopes and dreams have come true for you?

What happened when your hopes finally came true? Did you experience a big, dramatic change? Or did your life change less than you thought it would?

Which of your hopes has been "postponed"? As you've waited for your hopes to come true, has what you've hoped for changed? If so, why do you think that is?

think on it

First Thessalonians 1:2–3 says, "Every time we think of you, we thank God for you. Day and night you're in our prayers as we call to mind your work of faith, your labor of love, and your patience of hope in following our Master, Jesus Christ" (THE MESSAGE). Where is God calling you to be patient in hope?

How can you keep on seeking, asking, and knocking (Luke 11:9)? What does that look like for you?

Psalm 65:11 says, "Even the hard pathways overflow with abundance." What good things have come into your life while you waited? What unexpected blessings have you found along the way?

Act on It

Are you abounding in hope today? Are your hope, your faith, and your joy full to overflowing? Bubbling up? Splashing onto everyone around you? They can be! Even in hard times. Even on hard days.

In the space below, reflect on a blessing God gave you earlier in your life. How did that blessing open the door to others? Trace the way one gift led to another and notice how they connect. As you see God's hand in the details, let it remind you that when you seek God, hope abounds.

MY CUP OVERFLOWS WITH BLESSINGS.

PSALM 23:5

Day
21

Hope Sees

It's what we trust in but don't yet see that keeps us going.

2 CORINTHIANS 5:7 THE MESSAGE

God of our Lord Jesus the Anointed, Father of Glory: I call out to You on behalf of Your people. *Give them minds ready to receive wisdom and revelation so they will truly know You. Open the eyes of their hearts,* and let the light of Your truth flood in. *Shine Your light on the hope You are calling them to embrace. Reveal to them the glorious riches You are preparing as their inheritance. Let them see the full extent of Your power that is at work in those of us who believe, and may it be done according to Your might and power.*

EPHESIANS 1:17–19 THE VOICE

Isaiah 60:1
AMP

Arise [from spiritual depression to a new life], shine [be radiant with the glory and brilliance of the LORD]; for your light has come, and the glory and brilliance of the LORD has risen upon you.

Exodus 14:13
AMP

Do not be afraid! Take your stand [be firm and confident and undismayed] and see the salvation of the LORD which He will accomplish for you today.

Psalm 40:3

Many will see what he has done and be amazed. They will put their trust in the LORD.

Colossians 1:23

You must continue to believe this truth and stand firmly in it.

Psalm 31:24

Be strong and courageous, all you who put your hope in the LORD!

1 Corinthians 16:13–14
THE MESSAGE

Keep your eyes open, hold tight to your convictions, give it all you've got, be resolute, and love without stopping.

A NOTE FROM
Candace

Hope Sees

On day 17, we talked about how God's people celebrated when they crossed the Jordan River and entered the promised land. It was a day of rejoicing, a day of thanksgiving. A day that could have come forty years sooner had they adhered to hope and faith instead of fear and despair.

We see in Numbers 13–14 that God had brought the people to the promised land decades earlier, but the scouts they sent ahead of them took one look and freaked out! Yes, the land was filled with all the things God had promised. It was a fruitful land "flowing with milk and honey," a wonderful place to live (Numbers 13:27). But it was also home to some pretty fierce-looking giants.

God said not to worry about the giants; He would take care of them. Giants are no problem for Him.

And a few of the people believed Him. A few had eyes of faith and hearts full of hope. These people raved about the possibilities this new land offered. They rejoiced in the opportunities. They looked forward to the blessings. They couldn't wait to get started and see what God had in store.

But they got shouted down. Ridiculed. Rejected. Outvoted.

Fear won the day, and most of the people refused to take even one step farther into the promised land. They retreated into the desert, where God would spend the next forty years disciplining them—teaching them faith and trust, teaching them hope, and teaching them obedience.

And *then* the people were ready to discover all the wonderful things—and the amazing gifts—of the promised land God had wanted to share with them all along.

Their story is such a great reminder for us of the pitfalls and the possibilities in our own faith journeys. May God help us all to see past our fear into the glorious future He has called us to, a land filled with hope.

think on it

One time, God's people faced a vast army in a battle they were ill-equipped to fight. So they prayed, "We do not know what to do, but our eyes are on you" (2 Chronicles 20:12 NIV). Then God told them His incredible battle plan: He would fight for them! As it turned out, all they really had to do was show up and look to God. Have you ever done the same? Have you prayed and asked God what you should do?

Where has God been leading you? Is He calling you to a new city or job, to a new relationship, to a particular book of the Bible, or to something else? Why do you think He's leading you to this place?

What kinds of "giants" do you face? What problems or obstacles? What fears or doubts?

think on it

What has God told you about His plan for you? What is He telling you right now?

In the current battle you're facing, how are you keeping your eyes on Him?

How is hope helping you see what God has in store even amid giant challenges?

Act on It

Picture the giant you're facing in your life right now. Maybe it's a person or situation you find challenging—or something else. As you look it over in your mind, notice your thoughts and feelings. Pay attention to whatever worry, stress, fear, or doubt surfaces.

Now let's "reframe" it. Ask God to help you look at this giant again—this time with the eyes of faith, full of wild hope. Think of your giant as a challenge rather than a problem. And look for the possibilities, opportunities, and blessings in this situation.

Draw a frame below, then write or draw something inside this frame to represent your new view.

OUT OF THE FULLNESS OF HIS GRACE HE HAS BLESSED US ALL, GIVING US ONE BLESSING AFTER ANOTHER.

JOHN 1:16 GNT

Day
22

Hope Believes

Believe in the LORD your God, and you will be able to stand firm.

2 CHRONICLES 20:20

To all who received him, he gave the right to become children of God. All they needed to do was to trust him to save them.

JOHN 1:12 TLB

John 3:36

Anyone who believes in God's Son has eternal life.

2 Timothy 2:11–12

If we die with him, we will also live with him. If we endure hardship, we will reign with him.

Philippians 1:21
AMP

For to me, to live is Christ [He is my source of joy, my reason to live] and to die is gain [for I will be with Him in eternity].

2 Timothy 1:12
AMP

This is why I suffer as I do. Still, I am not ashamed; for I know Him [and I am personally acquainted with Him] whom I have believed [with absolute trust and confidence in Him and in the truth of His deity], and I am persuaded [beyond any doubt] that He is able to guard that which I have entrusted to Him until that day [when I stand before Him].

Isaiah 43:10–11

You have been chosen to know me, believe in me, and understand that I alone am God. There is no other God—there never has been, and there never will be. I, yes I, am the LORD, and there is no other Savior.

John 16:33
AMP

I have told you these things, so that in Me you may have [perfect] peace. In the world you have tribulation and distress and suffering, but be courageous [be confident, be undaunted, be filled with joy]; I have overcome the world. [My conquest is accomplished, My victory abiding.]

A NOTE FROM Candace

Hope Believes

Shadrach, Meshach, and Abednego found themselves in an impossible situation: They could dishonor God, deny their faith, betray their convictions, violate their consciences, and bow down to worship a massive idol built by the king of Babylon—all before an audience of thousands of people.

Or they could refuse. They could stand tall—at least, for as long as it took the king's guard to get to them and throw them into a fiery furnace, where they would die excruciating deaths.

Unless . . .

Unless God intervened. Unless God came to their rescue. Unless He showed up somehow, in all His mighty power, and performed a miracle.

They absolutely believed He could. They had the wildest of wild hopes that He would.

So the three young men told the king, "O Nebuchadnezzar, we do not need to defend ourselves before you. If we are thrown into the blazing furnace, the God whom we serve is able to save us. He will rescue us from your power, Your Majesty. But even if he doesn't, we want to make it clear to you, Your Majesty, that we will never serve your gods or worship the gold statue you have set up" (Daniel 3:16–18).

"Even if he doesn't," they said.

They understood their lives were in God's hands, and they believed He had the power to help them. They believed He had a plan, even if His plan was allowing their deaths right then, followed by heaven forever.

But no matter what they faced, none of it really made a difference.

There was just no way they would turn their backs on the God they knew and loved, the God they believed in and trusted with all their hearts. They knew He would never turn His back on them, so they would hope in Him as long as they had breath.

And that turned out to be longer than anyone imagined. Because they *did* get thrown into the furnace. God didn't stop that from happening. But He met them there and kept them safe, and then He brought them out alive and well. Stronger and braver and more full of wild hope than ever.

think on it

Psalm 18:29 says, "With Your help, I can conquer an army; I can leap over walls with a helping hand from You" (The Voice). What is the bravest thing God has ever called you to do? What has taken the most courage, the most faith, the most wild hope?

What did you hold on to during this time? What hope did you have? What promise from God's Word did you keep reading? What did you believe?

How did God show up for you in that moment or season? Was it the way you expected?

think on it

Think about how your situation resolved. Was it the outcome you hoped for? Why or why not?

What did you learn from this experience about yourself and about God?

How have you grown stronger, wiser, more courageous, or more hopeful as a result of going through this? How has your belief in God been strengthened?

Act on It

Take a few moments to create your own statement of faith today, like the declaration made by Shadrach, Meshach, and Abednego. Let it be an expression of your hope and trust in God.

If you need a little help to get started, you can use these prompts:

I believe that God . . .

I believe that I . . .

I believe that this life . . .

I believe that right now . . .

I believe that one day . . .

THIS I DECLARE ABOUT THE LORD: HE ALONE IS MY REFUGE, MY PLACE OF SAFETY; HE IS MY GOD, AND I TRUST HIM.

PSALM 91.2

Day

23

Hope Leads

Since we are living by the Spirit, let us follow the Spirit's leading in every part of our lives.

GALATIANS 5:25

Letting the Spirit control your mind leads to life and peace.

ROMANS 8:6

Proverbs 3:5–6
THE MESSAGE

Trust GOD from the bottom of your heart; don't try to figure out everything on your own. Listen for GOD's voice in everything you do, everywhere you go; he's the one who will keep you on track.

Hebrews 10:24
AMP

Let us consider [thoughtfully] how we may encourage one another to love and to do good deeds.

1 Timothy 4:12

Be an example to all believers in what you say, in the way you live, in your love, your faith, and your purity.

Philippians 4:4–9

Always be full of joy in the Lord. I say it again—rejoice! Let everyone see that you are considerate in all you do. Remember, the Lord is coming soon. Don't worry about anything; instead, pray about everything. Tell God what you need, and thank him for all he has done. Then you will experience God's peace, which exceeds anything we can understand. His peace will guard your hearts and minds as you live in Christ Jesus. And now, dear brothers and sisters, one final thing. Fix your thoughts on what is true, and honorable, and right, and pure, and lovely, and admirable. Think about things that are excellent and worthy of praise. Keep putting into practice all you learned and received from me—everything you heard from me and saw me doing. Then the God of peace will be with you.

A NOTE FROM *Candace*

Hope Leads

When I think of a person who consistently exemplifies wild hope, I think of Marilu Henner, my costar in Hallmark's *Aurora Teagarden Mysteries* series. I lived with Marilu for almost six months, and during that time I got to know her very well. She's one of the most optimistic and hopeful people I know.

Marilu has become like a second mother to me—she even plays my mother in the series—and I'm so inspired by her. She's a free spirit and has lived such a full life. Trust me: She has the most incredible stories!

Things haven't always been easy for Marilu. She's been through all kinds of tough times, including losing both her parents at a young age. She's been divorced twice but is now happily married to Michael, her "third and final husband." Early in their relationship, Michael battled cancer, and Marilu became his caregiver until he went into remission.

As an actor, as a woman, as a wife, and as a mother to two young-adult sons, she faces her share of challenges, but she chooses to embrace them with spirit and spunk. She has such a positive attitude. She actively looks for the good in every situation. Actually, she not only looks for it, but she expects it!

And when she encounters something negative, it's like she wears a coat of Teflon that protects her—the negativity never sticks. It's not that she doesn't have compassion for people who are feeling down, upset, or frustrated. But she doesn't let their moods or attitudes affect her own positivity.

Marilu is always saying, "Let go. Let God!" In other words, whatever you're worried or stressed or anxious about, let God handle it. He can take care of it. And He will take care of it.

I love that! I'm so inspired by her positive, upbeat approach to life, especially as she gets older—especially as I get older! I want to follow her example. I want to choose to be cheerful and optimistic and hope-*full*. I want to go through life with a smile on my face. I want to be the kind of person who encourages and refreshes others. I hope they feel good when we spend time together, that they are uplifted and inspired.

Just as I am by my friend Marilu.

think on it

Hebrews 13:7 says, "Remember your leaders who taught you the word of God. Think of all the good that has come from their lives, and follow the example of their faith." So who inspires you by example? Who lives a life of wild hope, a life of deep faith? Are these people in your circle of family and friends, at your school or workplace, or in your community? Are they men and women from history or Scripture? Make a list of those people here.

As you look over the names you've written down, consider what inspires you about these people. What is unique or special about them? What (if anything) do they have in common?

Do you consider someone in your life a role model or mentor? Why do you admire this person? Which of their traits would you like to weave into your own life?

think on it

Paul was intentional about setting a good example for others—not by being perfect but by doing his best to be obedient to God. He told believers in 1 Corinthians 11:1, "Follow my example, as I follow the example of Christ" (NIV). Who are you setting an example for today? Who are the witnesses to your life and faith?

How do you feel about the example you're setting? What would you like others to see in you or learn from you? How would you like them to feel when they spend time with you?

How can you be more intentional about cultivating your life as an example for others? What kinds of practices might help you become the good example you'd like to be?

Act on It

Let's practice taking Marilu's advice today: "Let go. Let God!" Psalm 55:22 says, "Pile your troubles on GOD's shoulders—he'll carry your load, he'll help you out" (THE MESSAGE).

Set a timer for three minutes, and make a list in the space below of all the things weighing on you right now.

Now take a few deep breaths and release these things to God. Ask Him to show you if there's anything you can or should do with the items on your list. Otherwise, leave them in His hands.

Again, let's follow Marilu's example by focusing on the positive. Set a timer for three more minutes, and this time, count your blessings. Write down as many things as you can think of that bring you joy or for which you are grateful today. And remember to praise God! Thank Him for the things on your list, and ask Him to help you notice other blessings as you go about your day.

PRAISE THE LORD, MY SOUL, AND DO NOT FORGET HOW KIND HE IS.

PSALM 103:2 GNT

Day
24

Hope Gives

The eyes of all look to you in hope; you give them their food as they need it.

PSALM 145:15

When God's people are in need, be ready to help them. Always be eager to practice hospitality.

ROMANS 12:13

Proverbs 3:27 *THE MESSAGE*	Never walk away from someone who deserves help; your hand is *God's* hand for that person.
2 Corinthians 9:7	You must each decide in your heart how much to give. And don't give reluctantly or in response to pressure. "For God loves a person who gives cheerfully."
Deuteronomy 15:10	Give generously to the poor, not grudgingly, for the LORD your God will bless you in everything you do.
2 Corinthians 9:6 *AMP*	[Remember] this: he who sows sparingly will also reap sparingly, and he who sows generously [that blessings may come to others] will also reap generously [and be blessed].
2 Corinthians 9:8	God will generously provide all you need. Then you will always have everything you need and plenty left over to share with others.
2 Corinthians 9:11 *THE VOICE*	You will be made rich in everything so that your generosity *will spill over in every direction.*
Philippians 4:19 *TLB*	It is he who will supply all your needs from his riches in glory because of what Christ Jesus has done for us.

A NOTE FROM *Candace*

Hope Gives

When we live with wild hope, it changes everything—even how we spend our time, our energy, our money, and all our resources!

We remember that Jesus said, "Life is not measured by how much you own" (Luke 12:15). Or to put it another way, "Life is not defined by what you have, even when you have a lot" (THE MESSAGE).

Our identity, our value, our purpose, our significance—none of these things comes from our possessions. We're not living for what we can accumulate in this life, because this life is only temporary. And we can't take anything—not one single thing—with us when we go. (And if we could see what God has in store, we wouldn't even want to!)

That's why Jesus says we should store up treasures for ourselves in heaven, not on earth (Matthew 6:19–21).

That's why we invest in what is eternal. We invest in God's kingdom.

We put people first—above things—because we know how precious people are to Him. We focus our energies on our relationships. We use our resources to bring hope, help, and healing to those who are hurting. We look for ways to show God's love to others. We support missions and ministries that point people to Him.

Jesus told us to "seek the Kingdom of God above all else, and live righteously, and he will give you everything you need" (Matthew 6:33).

We trust God to provide for us because He says He will! We rejoice in the freedom that comes from knowing everything we have is a gift from Him—and that there's so much more where it came from!

We don't live in fear. We don't stress or worry or obsess. We resist greed. We refuse to hoard. We know there will be enough for us. More than enough.

We train our hearts to practice gratitude and contentment.

We give and keep on giving—generously, cheerfully, hopefully—knowing we've been blessed to be a blessing.

think on it

What are your greatest needs right now? Where in your life do you need God's faithful, generous—or even miraculous—provision?

How has God met your needs in the past? What are some of the ways He has blessed you and provided for you?

Does the way you manage your resources right now reflect that your hope is in God? Do your choices demonstrate your faith in His faithfulness and your confidence that He will keep His promise to provide for you? Why or why not?

think on it

In Malachi 3:10, God says to those who honor Him with their giving, "I will open the windows of heaven for you. I will pour out a blessing so great you won't have enough room to take it in! Try it! Put me to the test!" How do these words challenge you? How do they motivate, encourage, or inspire you?

In Luke 6:38, Jesus says, "Give, and you will receive. Your gift will return to you in full—pressed down, shaken together to make room for more, running over, and poured into your lap. The amount you give will determine the amount you get back." How has giving your resources to someone else impacted your heart?

Have you ever given generously though you were lacking in that particular resource (time, money, or something else)? How did that situation work out? Where can you see God's hand providing for you in that time?

Act on It

Where has God blessed your life with abundance? What do you have that you could share with others? Think beyond money (although money is important to give!). Brainstorm ways you could use your time, your skills and talents, your wisdom, or your life experience to help someone else.

Could you knit hats for the homeless? Tutor a struggling student? Teach someone how to bake or how to budget? Give a night off to a caregiver or foster parent? Donate some of the things piled up in your closet or cupboards?

If you'd like to give more of your time or finances, what small sacrifices could you make?

Use the chart below to do some brainstorming. You may need to do a little research to figure out who could use some funds and how best to give on an ongoing basis. But try to come up with at least a few practical things you can do (or give) right away.

What I Can Give	Whom I'll Give To	When I'll Give It

THE GENEROUS WILL PROSPER; THOSE WHO REFRESH OTHERS WILL THEMSELVES BE REFRESHED.

PROVERBS 11:25

Hope Lives

Each generation should set its hope anew on God, not forgetting his glorious miracles and obeying his commands.

PSALM 78:7

The Lord is good. His unfailing love continues forever, and his faithfulness continues to each generation.

PSALM 100:5

Psalm 78:4	We will not hide these truths from our children; we will tell the next generation about the glorious deeds of the LORD, about his power and his mighty wonders.
Joel 1:3	Tell your children about it in the years to come, and let your children tell their children. Pass the story down from generation to generation.
Psalm 22:30 *THE MESSAGE*	Our children and their children will get in on this as the word is passed along from parent to child. Babies not yet conceived will hear the good news—that God does what he says.
Psalm 112:2 *THE VOICE*	Their children will be a *powerful* force upon the earth; this generation that does what is right *in God's eyes* will be blessed.
Isaiah 38:19	Each generation tells of your faithfulness to the next.
Psalm 145:4	Let each generation tell its children of your mighty acts; let them proclaim your power.
Psalm 145:13	For your kingdom is an everlasting kingdom. You rule throughout all generations. The LORD always keeps his promises; he is gracious in all he does.

A NOTE FROM Candace

Hope Lives

One of the things that fills me with wild hope for the future is witnessing the faith of the next generation. I love seeing my own children and the children of my friends and family put their hope in God and grow in their relationships with Him—especially now as they're becoming young adults, moving out, and making their own way.

It gives me hope to see them choosing *God's* way.

With all the other choices they could make, all the other directions they could take, they're deliberately, purposefully seeking Him.

For instance, my son Lev and my goddaughter Brooke both got their degrees in Bible and theology—not because they expect to go into full-time ministry but because they love God so much and want to know Him much better! They want to spend some in-depth, focused time studying His Word.

And there are many others like them! Young people are loving Jesus and living for Him in many different ways—using their gifts and talents to glorify Him.

They are strong in their faith, bold in their convictions, willing to make tough choices, and willing to make sacrifices for Jesus's sake. They are ready and willing to serve. Bold enough to take a stand. Eager to share the good news with their friends and family, with their school, with their youth group, in person, and on social media.

I know it's not always easy for them. But they're focused and committed and determined. The wild hope they have seen, the wild hope they have learned, now lives on in them. And through them, it reaches countless others.

Their example challenges and inspires me—and reminds me how contagious wild hope can be. It reminds me to share my hope more intentionally!

think on it

How are you sharing your faith—the "reason for the hope that is in you"—with the next generation (1 Peter 3:15 CSB)?

How are you setting an example for them "in what you say, in the way you live, in your love, your faith, and your purity" (1 Timothy 4:12)?

Who are your role models or mentors today? Why?

think on it

Scripture reminds us how important it is to "keep on growing in knowledge and understanding" as well as in God's love (Philippians 1:9). What are you doing to keep learning and growing on your own journey, and in your own relationship with Christ?

Think about someone you looked up to when you were young. What about them challenged or inspired you back then?

Now think about that person with your adult mind. Imagine what they might've been struggling with in their day-to-day that sailed past your attention. What do you admire about that person now? Why are you thankful for their influence on your life, even today?

Act on It

The psalmist prayed, "Even when I am old and gray, do not forsake me, my God, till I declare your power to the next generation, your mighty acts to all who are to come" (Psalm 71:18 NIV). There are so many ways to be intentional about declaring His power to the next generation—sharing your hope, sharing your faith, with those who come after you.

Here are a few ideas:

- Record your own faith stories or those of your family on video, in a scrapbook, or in a journal. Share these stories at family get-togethers, at reunions, or when you go on vacations together.
- Be open and real. Share specifically what God is doing in your heart and life in casual conversation as well as on social media.
- Invite a young person in your life to join you for coffee or brunch—your treat! Ask them about their life, invite them to share their story, and actively listen to what they tell you without offering judgment, criticism, or advice. Be willing to share your story with them too.
- Be extra kind, patient, and friendly with teenage cashiers.
- Send cards or texts to your children, your grandchildren or godchildren, and nieces and nephews on a regular basis. Let them know you're thinking of them, praying for them, and cheering for them! Acknowledge and celebrate special occasions.
- Volunteer to teach Sunday school or lead youth group, chaperone field trips, teach life skills or arts classes, foster, mentor, tutor, or work with at-risk youth.

Choose at least one of the ideas above and act on it this week.

I WILL MAKE SURE YOUR NAME IS REMEMBERED BY ALL *FUTURE* GENERATIONS SO THAT THE PEOPLE WILL OFFER YOU THANKS AND PRAISE *NOW AND* FOREVER.

PSALM 45:17 THE VOICE

Day
26

Hope (In)powers

I pray that God, the source of hope, will fill you completely with joy and peace because you trust in him.

ROMANS 15:13

Then you will overflow with confident hope through the power of the Holy Spirit.

ROMANS 15:13

Psalm 34:5

Those who look to him for help will be radiant with joy; no shadow of shame will darken their faces.

2 Corinthians 4:7

We now have this light shining in our hearts, but we ourselves are like fragile clay jars containing this great treasure. This makes it clear that our great power is from God, not from ourselves.

2 Corinthians 4:8–9
THE VOICE

We are cracked and chipped from our afflictions on all sides, but we are not crushed by them. We are bewildered at times, but we do not give in to despair. We are persecuted, but we have not been abandoned. We have been knocked down, but we are not destroyed.

Romans 5:3–5

We can rejoice, too, when we run into problems and trials, for we know that they help us develop endurance. And endurance develops strength of character, and character strengthens our confident hope of salvation. And this hope will not lead to disappointment. For we know how dearly God loves us, because he has given us the Holy Spirit to fill our hearts with his love.

Psalm 31:24

Be strong and courageous, all you who put your hope in the LORD!

1 Peter 5:10
TLB

[God] personally will come and pick you up, and set you firmly in place, and make you stronger than ever.

A NOTE FROM *Candace*

Hope (In)powers

The word *empowerment* is everywhere lately—in headlines, in social media posts, in self-help books, and maybe in your own conversations. It seems like everybody is talking about it. But I like the word *inpowerment* better.

Inpowerment is based on a concept the Bible talks about a lot: God's power at work *in* us. Ephesians 3:20 describes this power as "mighty"—able "to accomplish infinitely more than we might ask," or as one translation puts it, "superabundantly more than all that we dare ask or think [infinitely beyond our greatest prayers, hopes, or dreams]" (AMP).

So here's my definition of an *inpowered woman*: "a woman who derives her strength from God's limitless power within her."

I guess this resonates with me because I've spent so much of my life striving to do things in my own strength and winding up exhausted. And sometimes discouraged, frustrated, or hopeless.

But when I learned I could rely on God's power in me, my life began changing in amazing ways! I found new hope, new courage, and new energy and strength.

That hope itself—hope in God and in His Word—has been inpowering.

I've learned that "I can do all things [which He has called me to do] through Him who strengthens and empowers me [to fulfill His purpose—I am self-sufficient in Christ's sufficiency; I am ready for anything and equal to anything through Him who infuses me with inner strength and confident peace]" (Philippians 4:13 AMP).

That's why, although I'm still learning and growing amid my inpowerment journey, I'm excited to share this journey with you. I know you can be inpowered too. Our lives may look very different—our circumstances, our responsibilities, our challenges and opportunities, or the obstacles we face—but the same mighty God at work in me is also at work in you.

Our hope is in Him, and our power comes from Him. This is what we remind each other of; this is how we cheer each other on. Step-by-step, day by day.

think on it

What does being inpowered by your hope in God mean to you?

What Bible verses encourage you to rely on this inpowerment?

What are some things—big or small—that God has already inpowered you to do? What have you accomplished in His strength that you couldn't have accomplished on your own? List some of the little acts of faithfulness: kindness, gentleness, unselfishness, diligence, patience, or persistence. Then list what can feel like the big acts of faith: the huge projects you've tackled or epic obstacles or challenges you've overcome.

think on it

Look back at your list from the previous question. Which of these things was the hardest for you to achieve? Were they big things or small things? Daily things or once-in-a-lifetime things? Why do you think God planned for things to work out for you this way?

How do you need to be inpowered by God right now? Where are you tempted to rely on your own strength? What can't be accomplished without His help?

Matthew 5:16 encourages us, "Don't hide your light! Let it shine for all; let your good deeds glow for all to see, so that they will praise your heavenly Father" (TLB). How is God glorified by your hope in Him? How does it honor Him when you shine bright, even in hard times? How can you give Him praise and point others to Him?

Act on It

During your prayer time this week, light a candle as a reminder to let God's power shine through you. And take a few moments to finish the following sentences:

God, please inpower me to learn or to grow in ___________________.

Inpower me to begin ___________________.

Inpower me to be faithful to ___________________.

Inpower me to accomplish or to complete ___________________.

Inpower me to let go of ___________________.

Inpower me to overcome ___________________.

Inpower me to hope and trust and believe that ___________________.

THE GOD WHO SPOKE *LIGHT INTO EXISTENCE*, SAYING, "LET LIGHT SHINE FROM THE DARKNESS," IS THE VERY ONE WHO SETS OUR HEARTS ABLAZE.

2 CORINTHIANS 4:6 THE VOICE

Day

27

Hope Endures

As for me, I will always have hope.

PSALM 71:14 NIV

Those who trust in and rely on the Lord *[with confident expectation] are like Mount Zion, which cannot be moved but remains forever.*

PSALM 125:1 AMP

Philippians 3:13–14	I focus on this one thing: Forgetting the past and looking forward to what lies ahead, I press on to reach the end of the race and receive the heavenly prize for which God, through Christ Jesus, is calling us.
James 1:12	God blesses those who patiently endure testing and temptation. Afterward they will receive the crown of life that God has promised to those who love him.
1 Timothy 4:10	This is why we work hard and continue to struggle, for our hope is in the living God, who is the Savior of all people and particularly of all believers.
Hebrews 12:1–2	Therefore, since we are surrounded by such a huge crowd of witnesses to the life of faith, let us strip off every weight that slows us down, especially the sin that so easily trips us up. And let us run with endurance the race God has set before us. We do this by keeping our eyes on Jesus, the champion who initiates and perfects our faith.
Romans 12:12 *GNT*	Let your hope keep you joyful, be patient in your troubles, and pray at all times.
Colossians 1:10–11	All the while, you will grow as you learn to know God better and better. . . . You will be strengthened with all his glorious power so you will have all the endurance and patience you need.

A NOTE FROM Candace

Hope Endures

I think we all have certain hopes and dreams for our lives. I know I do! We make our plans, and we expect things to go according to those plans. But at the same time, we know life doesn't always work out the way we want. Things don't always go the way we hope or expect. And then we're disappointed, discouraged, frustrated, hurt, or upset.

Sometimes we feel this way because our expectations were a little unrealistic. Or we didn't have all the facts when we made our plans, so the plans went awry. Sometimes it's because we made a mistake; somewhere along the way, we fumbled or stumbled or failed.

Sometimes the circumstances are completely out of our control. As they say, "It is what it is." And *what it is* might be *really tough*!

What we *can* control, no matter what, is how we choose to respond.

We can remember that going through hard times helps us grow in character. We can look for the lesson—what the situation is teaching us.

Maybe we discover that we need to try something new—a new approach, a new attitude, or a new strategy. Or maybe we just need to practice patience and endurance. We know we'll grow stronger as we push through and keep on keeping on!

That's not to say that we don't feel the pain of our disappointment, or that we don't grieve our losses. We do. But we don't have to stay stuck in that place. We don't have to give in to hopelessness or despair. We can remind ourselves that God is at work, even in this.

When I need to reframe my situation, I remember this verse: "Dear brothers and sisters, when troubles of any kind come your way, consider it an opportunity for great joy" (James 1:2).

We may not know what God is doing yet. We may not be able to see where He's going with this. But we keep our eyes open and on Him, knowing He has good things in store for us. So with His help, we pick ourselves up, we get back out there, and we take the next step. We keep moving forward. With hearts full of wild hope.

think on it

Think about a difficult circumstance or season you've been through. Can you see an important life lesson you learned, or a strength or skill you developed as a result of persevering?

How did you pick yourself back up after a difficult season? When you think about how you handled that tough time, how do you feel about your choices? Do you feel proud? Do you wish you'd have done some things differently?

How have you grown spiritually—or come "to know God better and better" (Colossians 1:10)—through hard times? What have you learned about Him?

think on it

Where are you most challenged to persevere in hope right now? What situations or circumstances in your life today call for courage and strength and endurance?

What do you think God might be teaching you? Where do you sense He is leading you? What opportunities may lie ahead?

How are you keeping your eyes on God today?

Act on It

In Hosea 2:15, God told His people He would take their past failures, mistakes, frustrations, hurts, and disappointments and turn their "Valley of Trouble into a gateway of hope," leading them to a glorious future! And in Revelation 3:8, He promises He will open a door for us "that no one can close."

Imagine a doorway that separates where you are right now in your spiritual journey and where you want to be. Jot down what you hope lies on the other side—plus any steps you know you need to take to get there!

WE THROW OPEN OUR DOORS TO GOD AND DISCOVER AT THE SAME MOMENT THAT HE HAS ALREADY THROWN OPEN HIS DOOR TO US. WE FIND OURSELVES STANDING WHERE WE ALWAYS HOPED WE MIGHT STAND—OUT IN THE WIDE OPEN SPACES OF GOD'S GRACE AND GLORY.

ROMANS 5:2 THE MESSAGE

Day
28

Hope Rests

Wait . . . for God. Wait with hope. Hope now; hope always!

PSALM 131:3 THE MESSAGE

Why am I discouraged? Why is my heart so sad? I will put my hope in God! I will praise him again—my Savior and my God!

PSALM 42:5–6

Psalm 62:1
NIV

Truly my soul finds rest in God.

Micah 7:7
AMP

As for me, I will look expectantly for the LORD and with confidence in Him I will keep watch; I will wait [with confident expectation] for the God of my salvation. My God will hear me.

Psalm 62:1

I wait quietly before God, for my victory comes from him.

Psalm 46:10

Be still, and know that I am God!

Isaiah 51:5

My salvation is on the way. . . . Look to me and wait in hope for my powerful arm.

Jeremiah 31:25
NIV

I will refresh the weary and satisfy the faint.

Colossians 1:23
AMP

Continue in the faith, well-grounded and steadfast, and not shifting away from the [confident] hope [that is a result] of the gospel that you have heard, which was proclaimed in all creation under heaven.

Job 11:18
THE VOICE

Once again, you'll trust in the presence of hope; you'll scan *the horizon* and sleep safely.

A NOTE FROM
Candace

Hope Rests

Sometimes God asks us to wait. Wait for Him to work in our hearts and lives, or in the hearts and lives of those we love. Wait for His wisdom and direction. Wait for His provision or protection. Wait for help. Wait for healing.

Wait in *hope*.

We've talked about how this kind of hope isn't passive but active. There are all kinds of steps we can take, all kinds of things we can do while we wait. Good things, spiritual things, practical things.

But it's important to remember that sometimes the best thing we can do while we wait is to rest.

Because sometimes the situation really *is* out of our hands. There's nothing we can do but surrender it all to God, put it in *His* hands, and wait to see what *He* will do.

The Bible tells us God never grows tired, never grows weak or weary. But we do. We really need rest. Our spirits need rest. Our minds need rest. Our bodies need rest.

Without rest, it's hard for us to see clearly, hear clearly, or think clearly. It's hard to keep things in perspective or make rational decisions. It's hard to respond wisely when we're physically exhausted, out of emotional energy, or spiritually running on empty.

We practice good soul care and good self-care by making time to rest—by making time for things that renew, reenergize, or replenish us. Such things help us recover from a huge challenge or a hard day, helping us bounce back so we can be at our best.

This kind of rest doesn't have to mean bubble baths or spa treatments—unless that's your thing. It can be pretty basic: Take deep breaths. Drink more water. Move around a little. Stretch. Go for a walk in the neighborhood, the mountains, the woods, or the beach. Get some fresh air and sunshine. And get some sleep.

Lean in and learn to rest in God's character, His promises, and His presence.

Sometimes that's what all the waiting is for.

think on it

How would you describe your physical well-being right now? What about your emotional and spiritual well-being?

On a daily basis, how hope-*full* are you? What drains or depletes your hope? What fills or refills your hope?

When you're tired or burned-out, how do you respond to different people or situations that might need your attention? Do any warning signs alert you that you're nearing burnout?

think on it

Describe what "real rest" means to you. What fills your soul back up? What rhythms or practices help to revitalize your body and mind?

Listen to this paraphrase of the invitation Jesus gives us in Matthew 11:28–30: "Are you tired? Worn out? Burned out . . . ? Come to me. Get away with me and you'll recover your life. I'll show you how to take a real rest. Walk with me and work with me—watch how I do it. Learn the unforced rhythms of grace. I won't lay anything heavy or ill-fitting on you. Keep company with me and you'll learn to live freely and lightly" (THE MESSAGE). How does your heart respond to these words?

What do you imagine that keeping in step with Jesus, in the "unforced rhythms of grace," might look like in your life today?

Act on It

Earlier we talked about some of the things we can do to practice good soul care and good self-care while we wait on God and learn to rest in Him. Now write an action plan for how you can incorporate some of these healthy practices into your day. Then note how they impact you physically, emotionally, and spiritually. (Keep in mind this exercise is meant to be a helpful reminder to rest. We don't want this to become a burdensome to-do list. Be sure to give yourself lots of grace!)

GOD, PICK UP THE PIECES. PUT ME BACK TOGETHER AGAIN. YOU ARE MY PRAISE!

JEREMIAH 17:14 THE MESSAGE

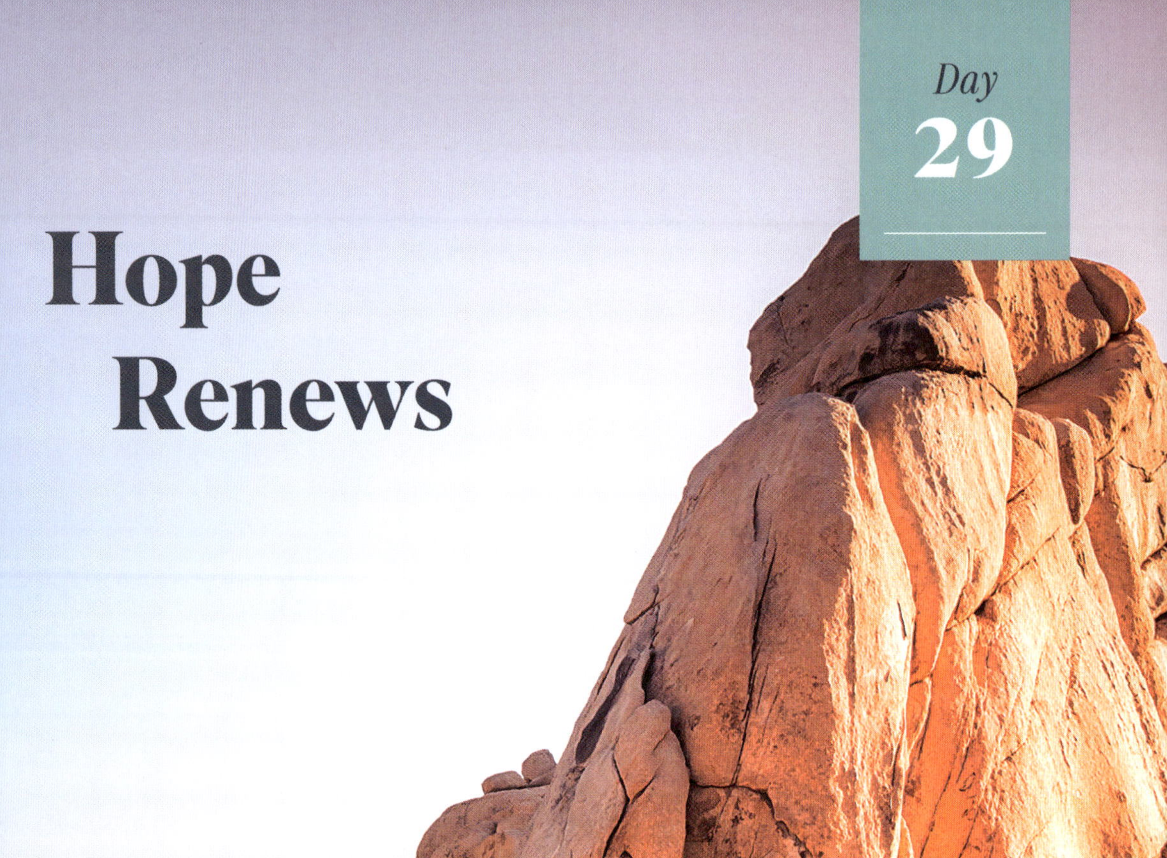

Day
29

Hope Renews

Though outwardly we are wasting away, yet inwardly we are being renewed day by day.

2 CORINTHIANS 4:16 NIV

We're not giving up. How could we! Even though on the outside it often looks like things are falling apart on us, on the inside, where God is making new life, not a day goes by without his unfolding grace.

2 CORINTHIANS 4:16 THE MESSAGE

2 Corinthians 12:7–10
THE MESSAGE

I was given the gift of a handicap to keep me in constant touch with my limitations. . . . At first I didn't think of it as a gift, and begged God to remove it. Three times I did that, and then he told me, "My grace is enough; it's all you need. My strength comes into its own in your weakness." Once I heard that, I was glad to let it happen. I quit focusing on the handicap and began appreciating the gift. It was a case of Christ's strength moving in on my weakness. Now I take limitations in stride, and with good cheer, these limitations that cut me down to size—abuse, accidents, opposition, bad breaks. I just let Christ take over! And so the weaker I get, the stronger I become.

Philippians 4:13
ESV

I can do all things through him who strengthens me.

Psalm 59:16

I will sing about your power. Each morning I will sing with joy about your unfailing love. For you have been my refuge, a place of safety when I am in distress.

Psalm 94:18–19

I cried out, "I am slipping!" but your unfailing love, O LORD, supported me. When doubts filled my mind, your comfort gave me renewed hope and cheer.

Psalm 89:8, 17

O LORD God of Heaven's Armies! Where is there anyone as mighty as you, O LORD? You are entirely faithful. . . . It pleases you to make us strong.

A NOTE FROM Candace

Hope Renews

One of the things I love about the Bible is that it doesn't hide from the hard parts of life. The men and women we meet in Scripture are often a mess!

Seriously, these people have all kinds of flaws, all kinds of weaknesses. At times they're proud or rebellious, stubborn or disobedient. As we read their stories, we see them making plenty of mistakes. They struggle to live out their holy callings and hold on to their faith (2 Timothy 1:9). They wrestle with worry and fear. Sometimes they lose hope, which leads them to really dangerous places.

But there's good news—for them and for us.

In 1 Corinthians 6:11, Paul wrote, "Some of you were once like that. But you were cleansed; you were made holy; you were made right with God by calling on the name of the Lord Jesus Christ and by the Spirit of our God."

Then in Romans 8:1–2, he wrote, "Now there is no condemnation for those who belong to Christ Jesus. And because you belong to him, the power of the life-giving Spirit has freed you from the power of sin."

This is our hope.

When we are weak, we are strong—because God is strong! He is at work in us and through us. When we struggle, when we stumble and fall, He catches us. When we cry out to Him, He helps us. He forgives us for our sins, all our failures and mistakes.

He heals us. He redeems us. And He restores us.

When we wrestle with doubt or fear, when we lose focus, when we're tempted to give up and give in to despair, God comes to our rescue. He lifts us up. He renews our hope. He renews our vision. He renews our courage and strength.

He draws us one step closer to Him—and then another and another. Day by day.

think on it

Isaiah 40:29 and 31 tell us, "He gives power to the weak and strength to the powerless. . . . Those who trust in the LORD will find new strength." The phrase translated to "those who trust" can also be expressed as "those who hope in the LORD" or "those who wait on the LORD" (NIV; NKJV). What are you trusting or hoping for? What are you waiting on God for right now?

What is God asking you to do with your life? What is His purpose for you?

Where in your life do you feel small or weak or powerless? Where do you need His strength?

think on it

Think about a character in the Bible you admire. Now think about the ways the Bible might describe how they messed up. How does it feel to know that the biblical heroes made mistakes too? Does it help you feel a little more tender toward yourself?

How do you think God can use your weakness for His glory? How could He use the situations in your life—even your mistakes—for good?

Psalm 55:22 says, "Cast your burden on the Lord [release it] and He will sustain and uphold you" (AMP). Deuteronomy 33:27 explains, "'The eternal God is your refuge, and his everlasting arms are under you." Take a few moments to write a prayer about whatever is weighing on you. Offer it to God. Release it to Him, to His care and keeping. Ask Him to give you courage and strength to do your part as you trust Him to do His.

Act on It

Take a look at this word picture in Isaiah 40:31: "Those who wait for the LORD [who expect, look for, and hope in Him] will gain new strength and renew their power; they will lift up their wings [and rise up close to God] like eagles [rising toward the sun]; they will run and not become weary, they will walk and not grow tired" (AMP).

Review the checklist below and answer the questions honestly. Then ask God to continue renewing your hope, especially in the areas you didn't check off the list.

IS MY HOPE IN GOD BEING RENEWED?

- When I pray, I expect God to hear me and answer me.
- I'm praying and memorizing scriptures more than I'm spiraling over negative thoughts.
- I'm noticing the beauty God created all around me.
- I'm joyful even when my problems aren't fixed.
- I'm trusting God with the circumstances I can't control.

HE FILLS YOU WITH GOOD *AND BEAUTIFUL* THINGS. . . .

HE MAKES YOU *STRONG* LIKE AN EAGLE.

PSALM 103:5 THE VOICE

Day
30

Hope Remains

Now these three remain: faith, hope and love.

1 CORINTHIANS 13:13 NIV

You are looking forward to the joys of heaven, and have been ever since the Gospel first was preached to you.

COLOSSIANS 1:5 TLB

Romans 8:18–21
THE MESSAGE

I don't think there's any comparison between the present hard times and the coming good times. The created world itself can hardly wait for what's coming next. Everything in creation is being more or less held back. God reins it in until both creation and all the creatures are ready and can be released at the same moment into the glorious times ahead. Meanwhile, the joyful anticipation deepens.

2 Corinthians 5:1–5
THE MESSAGE

We know that when these bodies of ours are taken down like tents and folded away, they will be replaced by resurrection bodies in heaven—God-made, not handmade—and we'll never have to relocate our "tents" again. Sometimes we can hardly wait to move—and so we cry out in frustration. Compared to what's coming, living conditions around here seem like a stopover in an unfurnished shack, and we're tired of it! We've been given a glimpse of the real thing, our true home, our resurrection bodies! The Spirit of God whets our appetite by giving us a taste of what's ahead. He puts a little of heaven in our hearts so that we'll never settle for less.

Hebrews 6:11–12
THE MESSAGE

Now I want each of you to extend that same intensity toward a full-bodied hope, and keep at it till the finish. . . . Be like those who stay the course with committed faith and then get everything promised to them.

Romans 15:13
THE MESSAGE

Oh! May the God of green hope fill you up with joy, fill you up with peace, so that your believing lives, filled with the life-giving energy of the Holy Spirit, will brim over with hope!

Hope Remains

Of all the things that give me hope, the greatest is the hope of heaven—God's promise of the glorious future that awaits those who are His! After all, "he has identified us as his own by placing the Holy Spirit in our hearts as the first installment that guarantees everything he has promised us" (2 Corinthians 1:22).

Ultimately, this is what we long for. This is what we live for. And yet it's beyond our comprehension. We can't even begin to imagine how incredible it will be. Paul wrote, "No eye has seen, no ear has heard, and no mind has imagined what God has prepared for those who love him" (1 Corinthians 2:9).

But Scripture—and His Spirit living in us—gives us hints, ideas, and images that we hang on to while we wait in hope.

We know we will live forever in the light of His presence—and that in His presence, there is "fullness of joy" (Psalm 16:11 NASB). We know that when we get to heaven, all our questions will be answered. All our deepest longings fulfilled.

There will be no more worry or stress, no more fear or pain. No more guilt or shame. No regret. The trials and temptations of this life will no longer trouble us. All our hurts and heartaches will be healed.

Death itself will be "swallowed up in victory" (1 Corinthians 15:54).

"Look," the apostle John wrote, "God's home is now among his people! He will live with them, and they will be his people. God himself will be with them. He will wipe every tear from their eyes" (Revelation 21:3–4).

No more grief. No more gut-wrenching goodbyes.

This world will pass away, but everything that's best and beautiful about it will be re-created in a new heaven and a new earth, where we will live together forever in God's love.

This is the deep, rich, wild, and confident hope He has called us to. It's the hope that remains through the hardest moments that life has to offer—the hope that stays with us, strengthens us, and sustains us day after day.

think on it

How do you imagine heaven? What do you long for? What do you most look forward to? Who is waiting there for you? What can't you wait to feel or see or do?

How does the hope of heaven impact the way you live today? How does it change your choices, actions, or behaviors?

How does the hope of heaven change your view of life's darkest moments?

think on it

In 1 Thessalonians 1:3, Paul wrote of our "unfailing, unwavering, unending hope in our Lord Jesus" (THE VOICE). Now that you've spent thirty days reflecting on what it means to live with wild hope, how would you describe it? What does wild hope mean to you personally?

How have you grown in your understanding of hope? Has anything changed? Have *you* changed? And if so, how?

Paul wrote that hope is one of three spiritual gifts that "will last forever" (1 Corinthians 13:13). Write a prayer, asking God to give you wild hope that will last a lifetime—and beyond.

Act on It

The Bible often describes us as travelers on a journey, as foreigners making our way through this temporary life to our true home in heaven. As you continue on your journey, what do you want to take with you from our time together? What souvenirs or mementos? (For example, favorite Bible verses, personal aha moments, or next steps toward living full of wild hope.) What tips or tools will you take with you on the road ahead?

Flip back through the pages of this journal to refresh your memory. Then take a few moments to record your highlights in the space provided below.

I'VE PITCHED MY TENT IN THE LAND OF HOPE.

ACTS 2:26 THE MESSAGE

You Made It!

And I'm so thankful you joined me on this journey.

Now keep going!

Keep holding on to your wild hope
as you walk with God each day.

A GUIDED PRAYER FOR WILD HOPE

Dear God,

Your Word says that as "the source of hope," You will fill me "completely with joy and peace" because I trust you. And because of that trust, I'll "overflow with confident hope through the power of the Holy Spirit" (Romans 15:13). Thank You for such a wonderful promise, God! Help me to always remember that You offer me hope, peace, and joy—no matter what I'm facing. Remind me of this truth, especially in my hardest moments.

Great is Your faithfulness, God. Your mercies renew every morning. You give me every reason to wake up each day with fresh hope. Today, help me give that wild hope to others, just as You have given it to me.

In Jesus's name, amen.

YOUR PERSONAL PRAYER FOR WILD HOPE

Dear God,

SUGGESTED BIBLE READINGS

The Bible talks *a lot* about hope and about what our lives can look like when we place our trust in God. I want to offer you more places to go when you need strength and encouragement during challenging times. For the next thirty days, let these verses guide your journey toward a deeper connection with the God of wild hope.

Day 1. Exodus 14:14–31
Day 2. Joshua 21:43–45
Day 3. Psalm 9:13–14, 18
Day 4. Psalm 28:6–9
Day 5. Psalm 33:13–22
Day 6. Psalm 39:4–7
Day 7. Psalm 42:1–2, 11
Day 8. Psalm 62:5–8
Day 9. Psalm 119:41–50
Day 10. Psalm 119:73–77, 81
Day 11. Psalm 147:7–11
Day 12. Proverbs 23:15–18
Day 13. Isaiah 26:3–7
Day 14. Jeremiah 17:5–8
Day 15. Jeremiah 31:7–17
Day 16. Nahum 1:7–8
Day 17. Habakkuk 3:2, 17–19
Day 18. Zechariah 9:9–12
Day 19. John 14:1–3, 12–14
Day 20. Romans 4:16–22
Day 21. Romans 5:1–5
Day 22. 2 Corinthians 1:8–10, 21–22
Day 23. 2 Corinthians 4:13–17
Day 24. Ephesians 1:15–18
Day 25. Colossians 3:1–4
Day 26. Hebrews 3:1–6
Day 27. Hebrews 7:19, 23–26
Day 28. James 5:7–11
Day 29. 1 Peter 1:18–25
Day 30. 1 John 3:1–3

PHOTO CREDITS

page 1: Hanna Aibetova/Adobestock
pages 2–3, 208: James/Adobestock
page 5: Westend61/Getty Images
page 7: sundaemorning/Adobestock
page 8: Wildroze/iStock
page 9: runlenarun/Adobestock
page 10, 207: Garratt Lobaugh
page 12: Alicia/Adobestock
page 15: Dorri Held/iStock
pages 16, 18, 21: Volodymyr/Adobestock
page 22: Wasim/Adobestock
pages 24, 27: JJ van Ginkel/Adobestock
pages 28, 40, 92, 94, 97, 100, 102, 105: jonbilous/Adobestock
pages 30, 33: youli zhao/Adobestock
page 34: mtilghma/Adobestock
pages 36, 39: Eric/Adobestock
pages 42, 45, 132, 135: Elena Ray/Adobestock
page 46: BCFC/Adobestock
pages 48, 51: Wally/Adobestock
page 52, 54, 57: A.N.Foto/Adobestock
page 58: Doug/Adobestock
pages 60, 63: Sara Edwards/iStock
page 64: sumikophoto/Adobestock
pages 66, 69: vinx83/Adobestock
page 70: joesayhello/Adobestock
pages 72, 75: lana/Adobestock
page 76: magdal3na/Adobestock
pages 78, 81: skywing/Adobestock
page 82: Schaefer Photography/Adobestock
pages 84, 87: Shane Cotee/Adobestock
page: 88: noframephoto/Adobestock
pages 90, 93: Hello Jess/Adobestock
page 94: jfr921001/Adobestock
pages 96, 99: Savvapanf Photo/Adobestock
page 106: PetraJPhoto/Adobestock
pages 108, 111: Richard /Adobestock
page 112: Scalia Media/Adobestock
page 114, 117: Gavin/Adobestock
pages 118, 120, 123: forcdan/Adobestock
page 124: gece33/iStock
pages 126, 129: Supitchamcadam/Adobestock
page 130: meg/Adobestock
page 136: veeterzy/Adobestock
pages 138, 141: thomsond/Adobestock
pages 142, 144, 147: Dmitry Vavilon/Adobestock
page 148: Tom Windeknecht/Adobestock
pages 150, 153: Garett/Adobestock
pages 154, 156, 159: Michal/Adobestock
page 160: avmedved/Adobestock
pages 162, 165: sheilaf2002/Adobestock
page 166: Travel Nerd/Adobestock
pages 168, 171: Yuval Helfman/Adobestock
page 172: Eldad Carin Ltd./Stocksy/Adobestock
pages 174, 177: ineffablescapes/Adobestock
pages 178, 180, 183: Juno/Stocksy/Adobestock
page 184, 205: kaelaimages/Adobestock
pages 186, 189: MaciejBledowski/Adobestock
page 190: DogoraSun/iStock
pages 192, 195: Alla/Adobestock
page 196–97: jessicahyde/iStock
pages 198–99: cceliaphoto/Adobestock
page 201: nickkurzenko/Adobestock
pages 202–3: ADDICTIVE STOCK/Adobestock
page 204: Silvy K./Adobestock
page 206: Sunny/Adobestock

ABOUT THE AUTHOR

CANDACE CAMERON BURE is an actress, producer, and *New York Times* bestselling author. She is beloved by millions worldwide as everyone's big sister, D.J. Tanner, from the iconic television shows *Full House* and *Fuller House*. She has starred in more than fifty Christmas and cozy mystery movies, and is a former cohost of *The View*. She is CEO of CandyRock Entertainment and host of her self-titled podcast. Candace is both outspoken and passionate about her family and faith and continues to flourish in the entertainment industry as a role model to women of all ages.

www.candace.com

Candacecbure

Candacecameron

candacecameronb

ONLINE COMPANION COURSE
Want more? I created an online companion course for you! Scan the QR code with a mobile device to see how you can join me for exclusive Scripture readings, stories, and a community where you can connect with other readers.